Print Edition ISBN: 978-1-956571-16-5
E-book ISBN: 978-1-956571-15-8

10 9 8 7 6 5 4 3

To the untold number of cooks who gave us their knowledge through the millennia.

"Our kitchens are filled with ghosts. You may not see them, but you could not cook as you do without their ingenuity: the potters who first enabled us to boil and stew; the knife forgers; the resourceful engineers who designed the first refrigerators; the pioneers of gas and electric ovens; the scale makers; the inventors of eggbeaters and peelers."

Bee Wilson, Consider the Fork

Table of Contents

Introduction

All living things need food to survive, but only humans have turned food into an art form. Only humans cook their food. We don't know exactly how it started. Archaeologists found remains of ash and burnt bone in a South African cave. Were humans cooking a million years ago? We don't know who cooked first, why they did it, or where it happened. We know cooking makes food more digestible. It killed bacteria that could cause food poisoning. The first cooking pots archaeologists have discovered were made and used in China 20,000 years ago.

But that's not why you wanted this cookbook. You wanted this cookbook because cooking makes food taste better! Even chimpanzees prefer cooked vegetables to raw vegetables. People experimented with herbs, spices, and flavor combinations even before they started cooking.

How about the history of the cookbook? Some of the world's oldest recipes come from Mesopotamian clay tablets. Made in about 1700 BC/BCE, they list ingredients with no directions for how to make the dish. For thousands of years, most recipes gave little, if any, instruction.

Instead, people learned to cook from the people around them. They already had the knowledge they needed to understand these mysterious recipes. In cultures with no written language, food traditions are passed from person to person. That means we can't always find the origins of a dish. How do we guess what people ate? Traditional dishes give clues. So does archaeology. Sometimes, we have only ingredients to go on. Writing a cookbook about the ancient world sure has a unique set of challenges!

In this cookbook, you will find recipes from all over the world. Some originate in the period from prehistory to about 400 AD/CE. Other recipes are based on traditional foods with ancient roots. When we say modern traditional in this book, we mean recipes that are only hundreds of years old instead of thousands. We believe experiencing cultures through food helps us make connections to the people of the past. Unless otherwise noted, these recipes are historically inspired rather than exact dishes. We adapted some for modern tastes, and of course, we adapted all of them for modern kitchens!

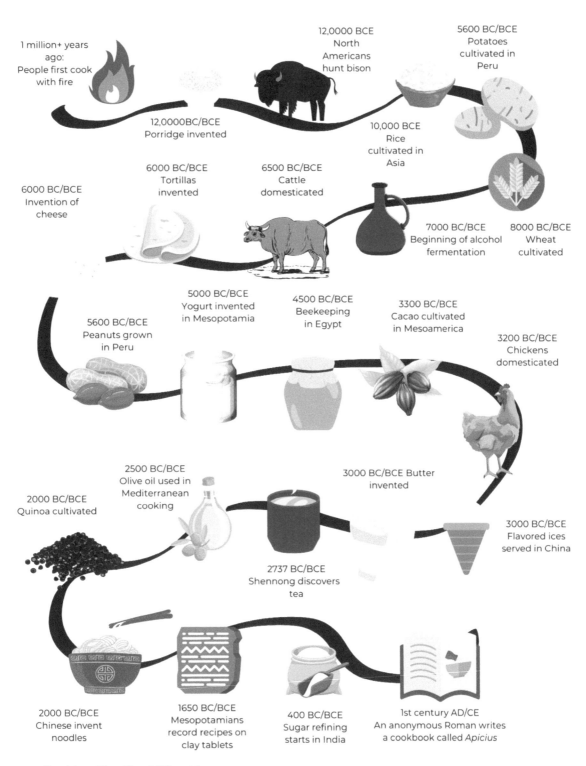

1 million+ years ago:
People first cook with fire

12,0000BC/BCE
Porridge invented

12,0000 BCE
North Americans hunt bison

5600 BC/BCE
Potatoes cultivated in Peru

10,000 BCE
Rice cultivated in Asia

6000 BC/BCE
Invention of cheese

6000 BC/BCE
Tortillas invented

6500 BC/BCE
Cattle domesticated

7000 BC/BCE
Beginning of alcohol fermentation

8000 BC/BCE
Wheat cultivated

5600 BC/BCE
Peanuts grown in Peru

5000 BC/BCE
Yogurt invented in Mesopotamia

4500 BC/BCE
Beekeeping in Egypt

3300 BC/BCE
Cacao cultivated in Mesoamerica

3200 BC/BCE
Chickens domesticated

2500 BC/BCE
Olive oil used in Mediterranean cooking

2000 BC/BCE
Quinoa cultivated

3000 BC/BCE Butter invented

3000 BC/BCE
Flavored ices served in China

2737 BC/BCE
Shennong discovers tea

2000 BC/BCE
Chinese invent noodles

1650 BC/BCE
Mesopotamians record recipes on clay tablets

400 BC/BCE
Sugar refining starts in India

1st century AD/CE
An anonymous Roman writes a cookbook called *Apicius*

Cooking: The First Million Years

Using this Cookbook

This book is a companion to Ancient History: A Secular Exploration of the World. For more about the civilizations covered in this cookbook, refer to that book.

Many ancient history cookbooks focus on the civilizations of Mesopotamia and the Mediterranean. It's an easy place to start since we have a lot of records about these civilizations and their food. But there is an entire world of food out there. We wanted to explore the food history of all the other cool civilizations we have written about at History Unboxed.

You can pair these recipes with a study of ancient history or you can compare them to each other. Compare flatbreads, porridges, or drin s across cultures! Throw a time traveling feast! Taste your way through time. In the sections featuring the history of food in each culture, there is a menu for a cultural feast. In addition to recipes, there is a list of fruits and nuts that were available in that culture. Serve these on the side or have them as an easy snack. These lists are not a complete list of ingredients. They are just a starting point.

Note: Wine and beer played an important role in many ancient cultures. Instead of including alcoholic recipes, you can drink grape juice instead. After all, grape juice is the first step in wine-making

Our recipes come from these regions and roughly these time periods:

Africa:

East Africa
Kingdom of Punt: 1493 BC/BCE to 1155 BC/BCE
Kingdom of Kush: 785 BC/BCE to 350 BC/BCE

West Africa: Ghana Empire: 300 AD/CE to 1200 AD/CE

North Africa
Egypt: 3150 BC/BCE to 1069 BC/BCE (Old, Middle and New Kingdoms)

Australia

Aboriginal Australia: 49,000 BC/BCE to 1606 AD/CE (1st European landing)

Asia

Jomon: 13,850 BC/BCE to 410 BC/BCE

Mesopotamia: 4500 BC/BCE to 539 BC/BCE (to end of Babylonia)

India
Indus Valley: 2500 BC/BCE to 1800 BC/BCE
Mauryan Empire: 268 BC/BCE to 232 BC/BCE

Empire of China: 221 BC/BCE to 220 AD/CE (Qin through Han Dynasty)

Mediterranean
Canaanite Culture:
Phoenicians: 2500 BC/BCE to 539 BC/BCE
Israelites: 850 BC/BCE to 586 BC/BCE

Ancient Greece: 507 BC/BCE to 323 BC/BCE
Roman Empire: 27 BC/BCE to 476 AD/CE

Eurasia
The Scythians: 600 BC/BCE to 300 AD/CE

The Americas

Ancestral Puebloans: 7000 BC/BCE to 1000 AD/CE

The Olmecs: 1500 BC/BCE to 400 BC/BCE

South America

Chavin Culture: 900 BC/BCE to 200 BC/BCE

Cookbook Development Journey -
A note from our historian

When we developed our ancient history boxes at History Unboxed, I loved the idea of bringing in food. The production schedule allowed little time for experimentation in the kitchen. We found a few recipes and snacks, but I wanted more. Since I was a kid, I've loved cooking. When I worked in living history, I got into historical cooking for the first tim . I learned how to prepare food like an 18th century cook. I read historical recipes and figured out how to actually ma e them. They aren't always as clear as today's cookbooks! I cooked over fires using griddles, cauldrons, and Dutch ovens. I even took part in historic cooking contests where the goal was always accuracy to the old recipes.

When I started this cookbook, I still had that frame of mind. I wanted everything to be 100% accurate and well documented. It was a fine idea. In theor . But the further I searched back in time, the more challenging it became. Ancient tastes aren't always in line with modern tastes. Many cultures did not leave behind written recipes. Archaeologists can sometimes figure out what people ate and something about their techniques - but that's not a recipe. It's one thing to know that ancient people ate millet. But how exactly did they prepare it? We may never know!

During the research process, I developed a new vision. What if these recipes connected us to ancient peoples? We can taste foods like those they ate. We can also acknowledge the connections built between then and now. Ancient peoples didn't go poof! and disappear. They are part of a rich tapestry of food tradition. Cuisine evolved as ingredients wove across the world. Some cultures continued from ancient times into the present. Other cultures faded or melded into new cultures, bringing their traditions with them. Another issue: ancient recipes don't always fit everyone's tastes today. I changed some recipes to make them fit modern American palates. You'll see that in the headnotes for the recipe.

In the end, I wanted to honor today's culinary traditions and connect them to the past. My recipes are inspired by the connections between past and present. They are not exact copies of ancient recipes or modern traditions. They are something in between. If you want a true taste of traditional international cooking, look for the experts. Check out a cookbook written by chefs within the culture. Go on a field trip to an international restaurant. Visit an international grocery store. Watch videos online showcasing traditional techniques. However you choose to learn more, have fun exploring!

Using this Cookbook

These recipes are intended for families to prepare together. We recommend always having an adult in the kitchen to handle knife work and hot items.

Explanation of Difficulty Level

1. These recipes do not require the use of sharp tools or high heat. Most children can prepare these recipes with minimal supervision or assistance.
2. These recipes have some knife work and may use the oven.
3. These recipes use kitchen appliances and may require cooking food at the stove. They may have multiple dishes cooking at the same time. They may also require more advanced knife work.
4. These recipes require advanced techniques and/or high-heat cooking methods.

Sourcing Ingredients

In these recipes, you will find a mix of common pantry staples and harder-to-find ingredients. Here are some recommendations on finding ingredients that are not available at your neighborhood grocery store.

- International Grocery Stores: Grains and flours are often on the shelves of international grocery stores. They are also a place to find condiments and less common produce. If you have an international grocery store nearby, check there first. They often have much better prices than internet retailers. It's also fun to wander the aisles and find new foods to try!

- Bob's Red Mill: Many products from this company are available from grocery stores, but they have an online storefront as well. They are a great source for whole grains and flours.

- https://www.culturesforhealth.com/ is a great website for dairy and fermentation starters and dairy supplies like cheesecloth.

- https://www.herbco.com/ is the place to find dried herbs and spices. Packages ship flat rate, so plan out your order carefully and take advantage of their prices.

Tools

Food Processor: A food processor makes quick work of jobs formerly done by mortar and pestle. You can use a mortar and pestle too. You will have a coarser result and stronger arms!

Cheesecloth, Butter Muslin, or Flour Sack Cloths:

These are great for straining, especially in making yogurt or cheese.

Dietary Needs

We recognize that diﬀerent families have diﬀerent dietary needs and we have worked to be inclusive of many diﬀerent diets. You'll see our recipes marked with the following:

 GF: Gluten Free

 DF: Dairy Free

 V: Vegetarian

 V+: Vegan

TIPS:

While adapting recipes for dietary needs may make them less historically accurate, we believe it's worth it to have the taste experience. Feel free to substitute vegan honey in any recipe calling for honey.

Gluten-Free Variations:

Recipes containing gluten-free flour were tested using Bob's Red Mill 1 to 1 Gluten Free Flour in place of wheat flour. Other gluten-free flours may have different results.

Ancient Cooking Techniques

How did people start cooking? They might have mixed foods together before discovering how to use fir , but it was fire that changed everything. t first, humans used fires created by natur . Forest fires left behind charred meat enjoyed by both Neanderthals and wild animals. Neanderthals heated pinecones on such fires. fter heating, the pinecones were easier to break open for the seeds inside. At first, early humans ept naturally started fires going or carried embers with them. The famous Ice Man, Otzi, carried embers wrapped in maple leaves inside of a birchbark box. By 790,000 years ago, humans had learned to make and control fir . They used it for roasting and drying. Around 400,000 years ago, a band of people camped along a lakeshore in Germany. They remained there for a few days while building fires to dry horsemeat to carry on their journey.

The earliest cooking techniques included roasting meat on a fir . Ancient cooks could either spear meat on a spit or wrap it in wet leaves and steam it in the coals. From there, people discovered how to eat grains and seeds. They pounded the seeds and then mixed them with water to form a sort of paste. When they put the paste on hot stones or in the ashes of the fir , it became the first type of bread. Flatbreads are almost universal across ancient cultures because they do not rely on the construction of an oven.

Open fire was the universal cooking element of the past. It remains common today, with around 3 billion people continuing to cook on open fires. et even with that single method of heat production, there is endless variation. People can boil water in a vessel over a flame or heat it by dropping in hot stones. Meat can be spit roasted, grilled in a pan, or boiled. Baking can occur in buried clay pots or in the ashes of the fir . Early cooks made cooking vessels out of wood, bark, hides, or animal stomachs. When filled with water, these materials do not burn over a fir . Later, people cooked in clay or iron vessels.

Preferred cooking methods varied by region. The Mesopotamians boiled their meat rather than roast it. They viewed using open flame as more primitiv . The Egyptians discovered the joys of fried foods. The Maori of New Zealand boiled foods in natural hot springs.

After cooking, food could be served and eaten in as many ways. Some might eat off of plates or out of bowls, li e in many European-based cultures today. Or they might use Āatbreads as a utensil, like in modern-day Ethiopia. Even today, people in many South Asian countries use banana leaves as platters. Regardless of where you went in the ancient world, one eating utensil would be missing: the fork. It wasn't invented until the 16th century AD/CE, so ancient people ate with knives, spoons, or their hands. They sat on the floor, gathered around fires, or reclined on couches. The most universal thing about cooking has always been the people. Cooking and eating have been social activities for millennia, as they are today.

Grains

Just about every culture that relied on agriculture had a staple grain in their diet. In the Americas, maize, or corn, fed people in both North and South America. Incas called quinoa "the mother grain." Millet originated in Sub-Saharan Africa. Barley and wheat grew all around the Mediterranean and in Europe. Rice ruled Asia from India to China. Over time, these grains spread in popularity. Today, millet is the sixth most popular grain in the world after maize, rice, wheat, barley, and sorghum. But millet dominated the ancient world. In Australia, Aboriginal people gathered grains from wild millet. They ground it into flour and used it to ma e bread.

By 2000 BC/BCE, people were eating millet in Japan, China, India, East and West Africa, and the Black Sea region in Europe. It's mentioned in the Hebrew Bible.

Grains show up in three major forms: bread, porridge, and fermented. "Cooked mush," or porridge, might have fed people 12,000 years ago! In South America, they made quinoa porridge three thousand years ago. In Mesoamerica, they cooked corn in water to make a thick drink now called atole. Chinese congee, or rice porridge, dates back to at least 2500 BC/BCE. Porridge was easy to digest and could feed infants and toddlers, but adults loved it too!

Early people also ground grains with a little water and cooked it on a hot stone. Even before people started farming, they were baking bread. The oldest evidence of bread dates back over 14000 years, in modern-day Jordan. Almost every culture turned their grains into a kind of flatbread in this wa . But do you know what happens when grains get wet and don't get eaten right away? They start fermenting to produce alcohol. Humans have been brewing alcohol since at least 7000 BC/BCE! It's possible that beer led to the invention of yeasted breads, as brewers learned to use yeast. Did some flatbread dough left out start to rise as wild yeasts from the air became active? Maybe the baker realized it tasted better that way. We don't know exactly, only that yeasted breads date back to at least 3000 BC/BCE in Egypt.

Today, we eat grains in many forms.

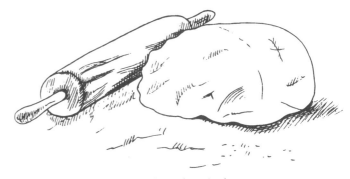

Definition Fermentation is a chemical process. Microorganisms, like yeast, break down one substance. This process creates compounds like carbon dioxide, lactic acid, or alcohol

BREAKFAST

Breakfast in the Ancient World

Fasting is the act of not eating. When we eat breakfast, we break our fast from not eating while we are asleep. Do you eat breakfast? In our culture, we often say that breakfast is the most important meal of the day. But breakfast isn't part of every culinary tradition.

Porridges date back to the Stone Age. Porridge might be the most traditional breakfast food of all. People still eat porridge today! Oatmeal and grits are types of porridge popular in the United States. It's easy to cook first thing in the morning and shows up in many cultures around the world. Other cultures did not have specific breakfast foods. In ancient Mesoamerica, tamales were both a breakfast and dinner food. Peasants in Egypt ate breakfast before the hard labor of the day. Beer and bread provided the needed energy for the day's work. They also ate fava beans and something like falafel for breakfast. The ancient Greeks called their morning meal ariston or akratisma. Tagenites, barley bread, and figs all showed up on Greek breakfast tables. Some Romans called their breakfast jentacalum. Bread, cheese, olives, nuts, and raisins all served to break their fast. Soldiers had porridge for breakfast. Other Romans felt that more than one meal a day was overdoing it and skipped breakfast. In Ancient China, breakfast took place by 7am, getting the day off to an early start. Before the Qin Dynasty, the morning meal took place a bit later, but was one of only two meals per day.

In the era before refrigeration, breakfast was a last chance to eat leftovers from the day before. Eating leftovers for breakfast is also easier than getting a cooking fire started first thing in the mornin

Mesopotamian Barley Porridge

Mesopotamians ate two meals per day: one in the morning and one in the evening. This porridge makes an excellent Mesopotamian breakfast. The wealthy would have enjoyed it sweetened with date syrup, while the peasant class would likely have eaten it without milk or other flavorings.

**V, DF and
V+ variation**

4 servings

**Level of
Difficulty: 3**

1 hour

Ingredients:

1 cup (200g) pearled barley
4 cups water
½ cup milk
Date syrup *(see page 221)*
or honey *(optional)*

Ingredients Tip:
*If you don't want to make your own,
you can find date syrup at many
international grocery stores.*

Directions:

1. In a medium saucepan, bring the barley and water to a boil. Reduce to a simmer and cook for about 45 minutes. The barley should be tender.

2. If any water remains in the pot, drain it off

3. Add the milk and cook on medium heat until the milk is absorbed.

4. Serve topped with your sweetener of choice if desired.

Dairy Free/Vegan Variation:
Substitute
coconut milk for
the dairy milk.

EGYPT

Egyptian Barley Meal Porridge

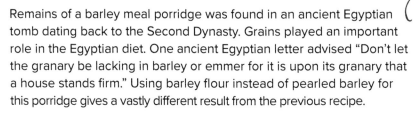

Remains of a barley meal porridge was found in an ancient Egyptian tomb dating back to the Second Dynasty. Grains played an important role in the Egyptian diet. One ancient Egyptian letter advised "Don't let the granary be lacking in barley or emmer for it is upon its granary that a house stands firm." Using barley flour instead of pearled barley for this porridge gives a vastly different result from the previous recipe.

DF; V

4 servings

Level of Difficulty: 3

30 minutes

Ingredients:

⅔ cup (100g) barley flour

3 cups water

⅛ teaspoon salt

Optional Toppings:
Honey; date syrup; chopped fruit

Ingredients Tip:
You can order barley flour online.

Directions:

1. In a medium saucepan, whisk together the barley flour and water until no lumps remain.

2. Bring to a boil on medium high heat, whisking constantly.

3. Reduce the heat to low and simmer for 20 minutes, whisking frequently.

4. Add salt and taste, adding additional salt if necessary.

5. Serve immediately with toppings.

MEDITERRANEAN

Puls Punica Phoenician Porridge

Puls Punica, a recipe for a spelt porridge, shows up in multiple ancient cookbooks written by the Greeks and Romans. Spelt is di~ cult to find, so we substitute wheat farina. Wheat farina is most often sold under the brand name Cream of Wheat®.

GF variation

1 servings

Level of
Difficulty:2

5 minutes

Ingredients:

1 ¼ cups water

3 tablespoons wheat farina

2 ounces goat cheese or ricotta cheese

1 tablespoon honey

Directions:

1. In a 1 quart microwavable container, whisk together the water and wheat farina. Do not use a smaller container, as the mixture may overflow.

2. Microwave on high for 1 minute and whisk again.

3. Continue to cook on high in 1-minute intervals, whisking in between, until the mixture is thickened.

4. Stir in the goat cheese until it is fully melted.

5. Top with honey and stir again.

Dairy Free/Vegan Variation: Substitute Cream of Rice® and cook according to package directions.

Millet Porridge

Millet was a staple grain throughout the ancient cultures of Europe, Africa, and Asia. A wild form grew in Australia as well. The Jomon of Stone Age Japan ate millet. So did the people of the Indus Valley, Mesopotamia, East and West Africa, Greece, and Egypt. It's somewhat interchangeable anywhere that people ate barley porridge. You can eliminate the milk or use coconut milk. In many places, they used just water. The Egyptians and Romans loved cinnamon. West Africans still love millet porridge with loads of warm spices.

GF, V, variation for V+ and DF

4 servings

Level of Difficulty: 3

35 minutes

Ingredients:

3 cups water
1 cup hulled millet (210g), rinsed
¼ teaspoon ground cinnamon
⅛ teaspoon salt
1 cup milk, non-dairy if desired

Toppings: honey, chopped dates, slivered almonds

Ingredients Tip:
If your local grocery store doesn't have it, you can find millet at some natural food stores and online retailers.

Directions:

1. Bring water, millet, cinnamon, and salt to a boil in a medium saucepan.

2. Reduce heat to low. Cover and simmer for about 20 minutes, until the millet has absorbed most of the water.

3. Uncover and bring the heat to medium. Add milk and continue to simmer, stirring often, for about 10 minutes. The porridge is finished when it is thick and creamy.

4. Add toppings and serve.

Variation:

In West Africa, the Hausa people make a smooth and spicy porridge with millet flour called Hausa Koko. It has ginger, cloves, pepper, chilis, and nutmeg. They serve it topped with sugar and with akara fritters on the side (*See page: 35 for recipe*). West African flavors inspired this variation.

In step 1, eliminate the cinnamon. Add:

1 teaspoon ground ginger
¼ teaspoon ground cloves
¼ teaspoon ground black pepper
¼ teaspoon nutmeg

Serve topped with sugar.

Jomon Buckwheat Pancakes

GF; V

The Jomon people gathered wild buckwheat. Despite the name, buckwheat is not wheat at all. It is not a grass, but its seeds can be used like grains. The Jomon people may have used buckwheat to make flatbreads. We used it to make pancakes for a sweet twist. Serve with fresh berries or strawberry sauce in honor of these ancient hunter-gatherers.

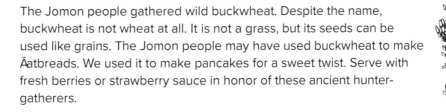

8 pancakes

Level of Difficulty: 3

Ingredients:

2 cups milk or buttermilk

2 tablespoons lemon juice *(omit if using buttermilk)*

1 ½ cups (180g) buckwheat flour

1 teaspoon baking soda

½ teaspoon salt

3 tablespoons unsalted butter, melted and cooled

3 tablespoons honey

1 egg

25 minutes

Directions:

1. Stir the lemon juice into the milk *(skip this step if using buttermilk)* and set aside for five minutes to thicken.

2. Preheat a skillet on medium heat.

3. Whisk together the flour, baking soda, and salt.

4. In a separate bowl, whisk together the milk, butter, honey, and egg.

5. Pour the wet ingredients into the dry ingredients and stir until combined.

6. Grease the skillet with about a half teaspoon of vegetable oil.

7. Measure out about ¼ cup of batter and pour onto the hot skillet. Cook for about 3 minutes each side, flipping when bubbles start to appear on the first side. Serve hot.

Strawberry Sauce

Ingredients:

4 cups frozen strawberries

1 tablespoon sugar

Directions:

1. Cook the frozen strawberries in a saucepan over medium heat until soft and juicy, stirring often, about 10 minutes.

2. Stir in the sugar and continue to cook for about 5 minutes.

3. Serve over pancakes or yogurt.

Acorn Cakes

Humans have been gathering and eating acorns from their earliest days. Acorns are high in tannins, which make them bitter. People around the world learned to soak acorns to leach out the tannins and make the acorns more palatable. Native American peoples across North America cooked with acorns. In California, some groups ate acorn mush called wiiwish or used acorns in soup with salmon, berries, and seaweed. Native Canadians made acorn bread. This particular recipe is inspired by the traditions of the modern-day Southwestern United States. You can use blue or yellow cornmeal, but the Ancestral Puebloans grew blue corn. These pancakes are not sweet like we eat our pancakes today! Even with leaching, acorns have a very strong flavor.

GF, V, variation
for V+ and DF

4 servings

Level of
Difficulty: 3

35 minutes

Ingredients:

1 ¼ cup (200g) acorn flour
1 ½ cup (140g) cornmeal
¼ teaspoon baking soda
⅛ teaspoon salt
3⁄4 cup warm water
½ cup honey + more for topping (vegan honey if desired).
Cooking oil

Ingredients Tip:
Acorn flour can be found at international grocery stores as it is also used in Korean and Japanese cooking today.

Directions:

1. Whisk together the acorn flour, cornmeal, baking soda, and salt
2. Whisk together the honey and water.
3. Stir the honey-water into the dry ingredients until you have a mixture resembling pancake batter.
4. Let the batter rest for at least ten minutes.
5. Heat about a teaspoon of cooking oil in a skillet on medium heat.
6. Use a ¼ cup to scoop the batter into the pan, working in batches if needed to keep the cakes from touching.
7. Let cook for about 2 minutes, until the edges start to get dry.
8. Flip over and cook for about 2 minutes more.
9. Serve hot and topped with honey.

Serving Tip: Use toppings based on the region you'd like to represent. Northeastern American peoples might use maple syrup and dried cranberries. Pepitas (pumpkin seeds) and sunflower seeds make great toppings too.

Magical Maple Syrup

Sugar maple trees grow throughout the mid-Atlantic and northeastern parts of North America. It is a good wood for carving and its bark can be used as a cough remedy. But in the northern regions of its range, the sugar maple has another gift to give: maple syrup. Maple syrup played an important role for many of the Native peoples in these areas. They shared stories about how people came to make maple syrup. When Europeans arrived, the Indigenous people showed them how to use the gift of the maple tree.

The Lenape (Lënapeyok) People

Axsìnamìnshi, the Sugar Maple, was suffering. Grubs and beetles buried underneath his bark. All their gnawing and chewing made him so itchy! His arms and fingers, beautiful with their leaves, could not scratch the terrible itch. A squirrel came running down one of his arms.

"Xanikw!" Axsìnamìnshi called to the little animal. "I have a terrible itching under my bark. Can you help me?" The squirrel hardly paused in his scurrying.

"Sorry, Axsìnamìnshi, I'm too busy!" Axsìnamìnshi sighed. Then he spotted the porcupine.

"Kawiya! I have a terrible itching under my bark. Can you help me?" Shuffling along, quills bobbing back and forth, the porcupine didn't stop.

"Sorry, Axsìnamìnshi, I'm too busy!" Then Axsìnamìnshi spotted a beaver gnawing on a nearby tree.

"Temakwe! I have a terrible itching under my bark. Can you help me?" The busy beaver just kept gnawing away until the sapling fell over and dragged it away without answering. Axsìnamìnshi sighed again. He asked the blackbird and the redbird, Tskennak and Mehokquiman, but they too were too busy to help him and flew away as fast as they had come. What would Axsìnamìnshi do?

Then, Papaches the Woodpecker landed on one of Axsìnamìnshi's branches. "Friend tree, you look as if you are suffering. What is wrong?"

"Oh Papaches, I have a terrible itching under my bark. Can you help me?" Papaches didn't answer but flew away. Axsìnamìnshi felt miserable. But then, Papaches came back. And he had brought his cousins with him. The four birds pecked and pecked and pecked until they had eaten every last grub and beetle. At least, Axsìnamìnshi felt relief! "Thank you my friends," he said to the birds.

"Thank you for the delicious meal," the birds said in return. They flew off with full bellies.

Some time later, there was a great drought. Papaches had not visited Axsìnamìnshi for a long time. But when Papaches landed in the maple tree's branches, Axsìnamìnshi could tell something was wrong.

"What is wrong, my feathered friend?" Papaches gave a tired shake of his wings.

"There has been no rain for so long. I am dying of thirst." Indeed, the little bird's voice sounded weak and strained. "Can you help me?"

"I remember how you helped me so long ago. Of course I can help," Axsìnamìnshi said. "Please, drill holes in my trunk with your sharp beak. My sap will flow and you can quench your thirst." The woodpecker did as Axsìnamìnshi said, and found that the sap was delicious. When the People saw the woodpecker drinking sap from the maple tree, they decided to try it themselves. And they have been tapping maple trees for their sweet sap ever since.

The Abenaki (Wôbanakiak) and Ojibwe (Anishinaabe) People

Long ago, life was easy for the People. The Creator had given them land to live on. Then he had filled it with plenty of animals to eat, plants to gather and grow, and maple trees. Maple trees were different in those days. To drink maple syrup, the People had only to break a branch off of the tree. Then the thick, sweet, sap would flow straight into their mouths. The weather was always beautiful and the People were happy.

Then one day, Gluskabe (or Nanabozho in Anishinaabe) was traveling to the villages. The Creator had sent Gluskabe to keep an eye on the People. When Gluskabe came to the first village, he found it empty. He went into one house after another, only to find the cooking fires gone cold. He went to the fields, only to find them filled with weeds. He went to the river, but no one was fishing. He went to the berry patches, but no one was picking.

Then Gluskabe heard a strange sound. It was a sort of moaning, gulping sound. He followed the sound to a maple grove near the village. There he found the People. They were lying under the maple trees, letting the sap drip straight into their mouths.

"You must rise and go light your fires," he said. But their bellies were so full of maple syrup that they felt sleepy. They barely seemed to pay attention to him at all. "You must go and fix your houses and tend your crops!" One young man stirred a little bit.

"We are happy to stay here and drink from the maple tree." Exasperated, Gluskabe went back to the river. He took one of the birchbark baskets from the village with him and filled it with water. Then he brought the basket of water back to the maple grove and poured it down the top of the tree. He returned to the river and filled the basket again. Again and again, he poured water into the maple trees. The People began to splutter and get up from under the trees. The once-sweet syrup was now hardly sweet at all.

"Where did our sweet drink go?" One of the People asked.

"Now you must work for it," Gluskabe said. "The sap will always be watery. And it will only flow one time each year. When it flows, you must collect it in your baskets. Then you will heat stones over the fire and drop them in the baskets to heat the sap. You must boil and boil and boil the sap until it is thick. Then you will have your sweet drink once again. The sap will flow during the time when there is no gardening to be done."

And so each year, at the end of the winter, the thin sap flows. And the people collect it and boil it for hours and hours until it is maple syrup once again.

Myaami (Miami) words for Maple Syrup Season
(Eehsenaamišipoohkiiyankwi)

Bark Baskets: wiihpišinaakani
Basket for storing maple sugar: wiiphšinaakana
Bucket: ahkihkwi
Maple sugar: siihsipaahkwi
Sap: ahsenaamišipowi
Sugar: paankosaakani
Sugar Maple: ahsenaamiša
Syrup: iihkisaminki
Water: nipi

To learn more about the ongoing tradition of Native sugar making in the Anishinaabe tradition, we recommend *Ininatig's Gift of Sugar: Traditional Native Sugarmaking (We Are Still Here)* by Laura Waterman Wittstock.

Food in Ancient Greece

Have you ever heard the word gastronomy? It means "the practice or art of choosing, cooking, and eating good food." (From the Oxford English Dictionary.) The Greeks literally invented gastronomy...or at least the word. An ancient Greek named Athenaeus wrote a poem called "Gastrologia. " That means "science of the stomach." Many of the Greeks wrote about food. They wrote cookbooks. They wrote about how to be healthy by eating the right foods. Clever cooks showed up in many ancient Greek comedies. Other writers left behind descriptions of dinner parties.

This means we know a lot about how the Greeks ate. We know so much it's hard to narrow it all down! They liked a combination of sweet and sour flavors. They cooked meat and fish with three or four herbs or spices. Many philosophers, including Plato and Pythagoras, encouraged people to eat a vegetarian diet. The poorer people often followed this advice, even if it was not by choice. For everyone, grains and pulses (dry

Phoenician Flatbread

Gastris

Cheese of the Herd

Cucumber Salad

Marinated Beets

Split Pea Soup

How do we know? The ancient Greeks left behind plays, histories, and other written records. Archaeologists have studied Greek historic sites for years. Sculptures and pottery depict various scenes of life.

beans and lentils) made up about 80 percent of their diet. Barley was the most common grain. They used it to make bread and porridge. They made vegetables into soup or boiled and mashed them.

Today, a Greek salad includes lettuce, tomato, feta cheese, olives, and red onions. The ancient Greeks didn't have tomatoes. Those only grew in the Americas back then. But they had all the other ingredients. A salad with a simple dressing of red wine vinegar, oregano, and garlic would be right up their alley! Cheese was actually essential. It was a good way to preserve milk from sheep, cows, and goats. They also made yogurt. Yogurt and cheese are both fermented products. Fermentation is one way to make food last longer without refrigeration.

The Greeks sweetened their sauces and desserts with honey and fruit. Later, they learned about crystallized sugar from India thanks to Alexander the Great. The Greeks were glad to adopt new ingredients as they came along. Dates didn't grow in Greece, but were a popular import. Olives did much better in rocky Greece, growing in the same hills where they grazed sheep and goats.

At Greek dinner tables, men and women ate apart. Wealthy people had servants cut up their food, and then they ate with their hands, lying down and relaxing. The less wealthy sat on the floor. With over 70 kinds of known Greek breads, they sometimes used flatbreads as plates. After a feast, servants cleared away the dinner table and then brought in a clean "second table" for dessert. They enjoyed sweet desserts, just like we do today.

Ancient Greek Menu:

Breakfast:
Puls Punica: *p.19*
Millet Porridge: *p.21*
Tagenites: *p.31*

Snack:
Dried apples: *p.42*
Yogurt (with honey): *p.58*
Raisins: *p.41*
Roasted chestnuts: *p.47*
Cheese of the Herd: *p.55*

Dinner:
Phoenician Flatbread: *p.65*
Marinated beets: *p.82*
Cucumber salad: *p.73*
Athenian split pea soup: *p.113*

Dessert:
Gastris: *p.173*

Drinks:
Grape juice: *p.196*

Fruits and Nuts
Almonds
Apples
Apricots
Bananas *(tasted by Alexander the Great)*
Dates
Figs
Grapes
Melons
Olives
Peaches *(Brought back by Alexander the Great)*
Plums
Pomegranates
Raspberries
Walnuts

"Have you ever watched to see the hot pancakes steaming as when you pour honey on them?"

Magnes, Athenian poet, 5th century BC/BCE

Greek Tagenites

These delightful pancakes are easy to make, delicious, and historically accurate! The Greeks sometimes topped them with yogurt as well as honey.

V, DF, V+, and GF variation

10-12 pancakes

Level of Difficulty: 3

1 hour

Ingredients:

2 cups warm water *(slightly warmer than body temperature but not hot, about 100 degrees)*

1 ½ teaspoons dry yeast

½ cup olive oil, plus more for cooking

2 tablespoons sugar

1 teaspoon salt

1 ¾ cups (400g) all-purpose flour

Honey, almonds, walnuts, or yogurt for topping.

GF Variation

Use 1 ¾ cups (420g) gluten-free flour. Reduce olive oil to ⅓ cup. Cook for 3 minutes on each side.

Directions:

1. Dissolve the yeast in the water until it looks pasty.

2. In a large boil, mix the water, yeast, oil, sugar, and salt.

3. Add the flour to the liquid and whisk until smooth.

4. Let the batter sit for 20-30 minutes in a warm place *(around 70 degrees)*.

5. Put a cookie sheet in the oven and preheat to the oven's lowest temperature.

6. Heat a skillet on medium heat with just enough oil to coat the bottom.

7. When the pan is hot, use a ¼ cup measure to pour batter into the pan. You can cook more than one at a time as long as they don't touch.

8. Cook until the bottom is golden brown and the edges start to look dry, about 2 minutes.

9. Flip the pancake and cook another 2 minutes until that side is golden brown. Keep finished pancakes warm in the oven.

10. Pour honey on the hot pancakes and watch it steam. Add other toppings as desired.

INDIA

Mauryan Malpua Pancakes

According to legend, Chandragupta Maurya was walking around his military camp discussing strategy with one of his commanders. He saw a young mother serving malpua, barley pancakes, to her son. The young boy discarded the edges of the pancake. Chandragupta realized that just as the boy discarded the edges of the pancake, he had left his frontier borders undefended. He changed his strategy to better defend his borders so his enemies could not surround him.

DF; V; V+

4 servings

Level of Difficulty: 3

30 minutes

Ingredients:

⅓ cup brown sugar or jaggery
1 ⅓ cup dairy or non-dairy milk
1 ½ cups (235g) barley flour
¾ teaspoon fennel seeds
¼ teaspoon ground black pepper
⅛ teaspoon salt
1 tablespoons ghee, butter, or olive oil plus additional for cooking
Honey for topping (optional)

Ingredients Tip:
Barley flour can be ordered on-line.

Directions:

1. Whisk together the milk and brown sugar.

2. Pour the barley flour into a large bowl. Whisk in the spices.

3. Gradually whisk in the milk mixture.

4. Whisk in the butter.

5. Heat the pan and melt about a tablespoon of butter or ghee.

6. Use a ladle to pour the batter into the pan until you have a pancake about five inches across.

7. Cook for about three minutes, then carefully flip over and cook for about a minute more. The pancakes should be reddish brown and crisp around the edges.

8. Served topped with honey.

Punt Pancakes

These savory pancakes are made from chickpea (garbanzo bean) flour. People have been domesticating chickpeas for 11,000 years and were popular in Egypt, the Middle East, and India thousands of years ago. It's likely that they made their way to Punt as well. Today, these pancakes are popular in Somalia where they often accompany curry dishes. The modern version is spicy, flavored with chili powder or red pepper flakes, but these ingredients were unknown in the area during ancient times. likely that they made their way to Punt as well. Today, these pancakes are popular in Somalia where they often accompany curry dishes. The modern version is spicy, flavored with chili powder or red pepper flakes, but these ingredients were unknown in the area during ancient times.

GF; DF; V; V+   10 pancakes   Level of Difficulty: 3   1 hour

Ingredients:

1 cup (125g) chickpea flour

1 teaspoon ground cumin

1 teaspoon ground turmeric

1 teaspoon salt

1 cups water

1 tablespoon olive oil

Ingredients Tip:

Chickpea flour can be found at international grocery stores under its Indian name, besan. It is also available from online retailers.

Directions:

1. Whisk together the flour and spices.

2. Slowly pour in the water, whisking as you pour. Whisk until the batter is smooth.

3. Heat about a teaspoon of oil in a skillet over medium heat.

4. Ladle ¼ cup of batter into the skillet and cook for 1-2 minutes on each side. They should be golden brown on each side.

5. Repeat with remaining batter, adding oil a teaspoon at a time as needed to keep the pancakes from sticking. Serve warm.

Ghanian Akara Fritters

Deep fried spicy fritters made with black-eyed peas or cowpeas are a popular breakfast food in West Africa today. It is a complicated process involving soaking and dehulling beans, pureeing them with spices, whisking the batter to incorporate air and make the fritters fluffy, and then deep frying the batter in hot oil. They are often served with hausa koko , or millet porridge. For this recipe, we have taken the ancient flavors used in this dish and simplified the process.

Ingredients:

GF; DF; V; Vegan

4 fritters

Level of
Difficulty: 2

20 minutes

1 can black-eyed peas, drained and rinsed

1 teaspoon ground ginger

½ teaspoon onion powder

Directions:

1. Preheat the oven to 375 degrees and grease a baking sheet.

2. Using a fork or potato masher, smash the peas until they are mostly pureed.

3. Stir in the ginger and onion powder.

4. Use a ¼ cup measure to scoop the mixture, pressing it into the cup until it holds its shape.

5. Plop the mixture onto the greased baking sheet. Repeat for the remaining mixture.

6. Use a spatula to press the patties into ¾ inch high discs.

7. Bake for 15-20 minutes on each side, until the edges are crispy and the tops are brown.

8. Serve warm.

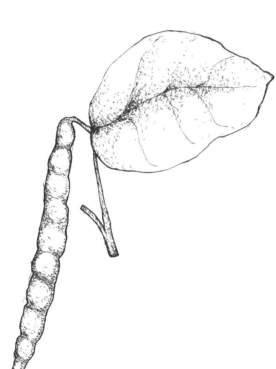

SNACKS
AND
BREADS

Lunches and Snacks in the Ancient World

Nowadays, we usually eat a light meal around the middle of the day. We call this meal lunch. But did you know that lunch is the newest meal? The midday meal used to be dinner!

The word "lunch" only dates back to 1786, and is short for "luncheon." Luncheon originally meant "thick piece" or "hunk." It may have referred to a piece of bread or meat. Even lunch had this same meaning at first. It did 't mean a midday meal until at least 1817!

The word "snack" is a bit older. It is a Dutch word from the 1300s. "Snacken" meant "snatch" or "snap." By the early 1800s, snacking meant eating something small and quick in between meals. Even without the name, snacking is an ancient tradition.

MESOPOTAMIA, MEDITERRANEAN, NORTH AMERICA

Oven-Dried Raisins

Historians think that people first ate raisins after discovering dried out grapes on the vine. Ancient peoples dried their raisins in the sun, but oven-dried raisins are yummy too. People in Mesopotamia, Egypt, Greece, and Rome cultivated grapes for raisins, wine, and fresh fruit. In North America, Native American peoples gathered wild grapes. They sometimes used grape leaves to wrap their food and steam it in coals. These raisins are much better than store-bought raisins. Snack on them or use them in other ancient recipes.

GF, V, DF, and V+

2 cups raisins

Level of
Difficulty: 2

10+ hours

Ingredients:

1 lb. grapes

Olive oil

Directions:

1. Preheat the oven to 170 degrees.

2. Wash the grapes and remove the stems. Discard any mushy or moldy grapes.

3. Drizzle a very thin layer of olive oil on a sheet pan.

4. Spread the grapes out on the pan.

5. Put in the oven and cook for at least 10 hours. Your time will vary depending on the size of your grapes and how dry you want them to be.

6. Store in the refrigerator for up to three weeks.

EURASIA, MIDDLE EAST AND MEDITERRANEAN

Dried Apples

Drying was one of the earliest methods of food preservation and was used by hunter gatherers. In Eurasia, Mesopotamia, Egypt, and the Mediterranean, people from all walks of life snacked on dried apples. They would have dried them in the sun, but you can also use your oven. Apples have remained popular and today there are over 10,000 diﬀerent kinds of apples.

GF; V+; DF; Vegan

4 servings

Level of Difficulty: 2

6 ½ hours

Ingredients:

2 quarts water

2 tablespoons apple cider vinegar

4 apples

Special Equipment:
Oven-safe wire racks

Directions:

1. Combine the water and apple cider vinegar in a large bowl.

2. Preheat the oven to 170 degrees.

3. Wash and peel the apples.

4. Core the apple and cut each apple into ¼ inch slices. Drop the slices into the vinegar water as you go to keep them from turning brown.

5. Place oven-safe wire racks on top of baking sheets. Lay the apples on the racks, making sure to leave space in between each slice.

6. Bake the apple slices for about 6 hours, checking on them about every 15 minutes after the 5 hour mark. Remove when chewy.

7. Let cool for 20 minutes and then put in a storage container. Store in the refrigerator for up to a week *(in case of residual moisture)*.

Popcorn

Popcorn has a long history. People have been eating popcorn since 3600 BC/BCE in Mexico and 4700 BC/BCE in Peru. In the 1800s, Americans ate it with milk and sweetener as a breakfast cereal. And of course, today it's often the movie snack of choice. Feel free to add modern toppings like butter or salt after tasting it plain like the ancients ate it.

GF; DF; V; V+

4 cups

Level of
Difficulty: 1

2 minutes

Ingredients:

2 tablespoons unpopped popcorn kernels.

Special Equipment:

Paper lunch bag

Directions:

1. Put the popcorn kernels in a paper bag and roll down the top of the bag a couple of times.

2. Put the bag in the microwave and cook on high for about two minutes.

3. The popcorn is done when the pops are about 2 seconds apart. Stop cooking at this point or the popcorn will burn.

4. Remove the bag carefully and open facing away from you.

WEST AFRICA
Fried Plantains

Plantains are really just a type of banana, but a variety that is usually cooked rather than eating raw. Bananas originated in Southeast Asia but spread to nearby areas early on. They were eaten on the African continent by 1000 BC/BCE after their arrival in Madagascar. Alexander the Great may have eaten bananas during his time in India and even taken some on the return journey. When the Moors invaded Spain and North Africa, they introduced bananas to those regions as well. Today the world's biggest banana consumers are Ugandans (in plantain form) and Americans. Fried Plantains are a popular snack in many West African countries today. Dodo is the Yoruba word for Fried Plantains.

GF; DF; V; V+

2 servings

Level of
Difficulty: 3

20 minutes

Ingredients:

2 ripe yellow plantains.
2-3 tablespoons cooking oil

Ingredients Tip:
When choosing plantains, look for plantains with yellow skin and a lot of brown or black spots. Even all dark plantains are still good as long as they feel firm to the touch! The riper they are, the more sugar there is to caramelize!

Directions:

1. To peel plantains, use a sharp knife to cut down the entire length of the peel. Instead of peeling top to bottom like a banana, peel by pulling the strips from side to side.

2. Cut the plantains into ¼ inch diagonal slices.

3. Add just enough oil to a skillet to coat the bottom and heat on medium until the oil is just shimmering.

4. Working in batches, use a spatula to transfer the plantain slices to the skillet, leaving space between the slices. Cook for about 1 ½ minutes on each side, until they are starting to caramelize and soften. Remove to a paper-towel lined plate and repeat until all the plantains are cooked. Lower the heat as needed to keep the plantains from burning.

Food in Ancient Japan

The Jomon civilization of Japan lasted from around 13,000 BC/BCE to 410 BC/BCE. The Jomon people were hunters and gatherers. They were among the earliest people to make pottery. The Jomon used their clay pots for food storage and cooking.

Japan had an abundance of wild foods and what people ate varied from region to region. Many people lived near the ocean or rivers. Jomon fishers used harpoons, nets, baskets and hooks to catch fish and sea mammals. They gathered shellfish like clams. They cooked their catch in hearty seafood stews. They also liked steamed oysters, exactly like many people enjoy today. They also dried or smoked fish to make it last longer. The Japanese didn't invent sushi for a few thousand more years, but the Jomon still liked raw fish.

In forests, the Jomon gathered nuts like acorns, chestnuts, walnuts, and hazelnuts. They ground the nuts into flour to make dishes like acorn dumplings and chestnut cookies. The acorn dumplings went into a stew prepared with root vegetables and herbs, cooked for hours in a clay pot. The Jomon collected seeds and grains from wild grasses. They harvested buckwheat, rice, wheat, and millet. Animals roamed the forests too. Hunters brought back deer, boar, bear, hare, pheasant, duck, and raccoon dog (a type of fox).

They drank wine made from wild elderberries, grapes, and mulberries.

They likely ate with their hands. Chopsticks didn't become popular in Japan until the 8th century AD/CE.

How do we know what they ate? Archaeologists studied residues in food pots, shell middens (trash piles), and food remains.

Ancient Japan Menu:

Snacks:
Roasted chestnuts: *p.47*

Dinner:
Millet flatbread: *p.61*
Seafood stew: *p.117*

Dessert:
Chestnut cookies: *p.171*

Drinks:
Grape juice: *p.196*

Fruits and Nuts:
Chestnuts
Grapes
Hazelnuts
Peaches
Raspberries
Walnuts

JAPAN

Roasted Chestnuts

Chestnuts have been a vital food around the world for thousands of years, including for the Jomon people of Japan. Modern Japanese cooks serve candied chestnuts with mashed sweet potatoes for New Year's. In Ancient Greece, they were dedicated to the god Zeus and preserved in jars of honey. The Romans made chestnut broth. In the present-day United States, Native Americans used chestnuts to make Āour.

GF, Vegan, V+

4 servings

Level of
Difficulty: 3

30 minutes

Ingredients:

1 pound chestnuts, raw and unpeeled

Ingredients Tip:
They are sold seasonally in November and December at most grocery stores, but can sometimes be ordered online during the rest of the year.

Directions:

1. In a medium saucepan, whisk together the barley Āour and water until no lumps remain.

2. Bring to a boil on medium high heat, whisking constantly.

3. Reduce the heat to low and simmer for 20 minutes, whisking frequently.

4. Add salt and taste, adding additional salt if necessary.

5. Serve immediately with toppings.

Murmura Chivda

Puffed rice, or Muri, has a centuries old history in India, China, and nearby regions. It dates back to at least 1000 AD/CE in China, but some believe it dates all the way back to ancient times in India based on references in Sanskrit religious texts. Traditional murmura chivda is sweet, salty, and spicy. We've simplified the ingredients and left off the hot peppers that were not available to the people of Ancient India.

GF; DF; V; V+

3 cups

Level of
Difficulty: 2

50 minutes

Ingredients:

2 ½ cups murmura (puffed rice)

2 tablespoons sliced almonds

1 can chickpeas, drained and rinsed

¼ cup raisins

2 tablespoons unsweetened dried coconut

2 tablespoons sugar

¼ teaspoon salt

Ingredients Tip:

Murmura can be found at many international markets. If you don't have one nearby, you can substitute crisped rice cereal. It's slightly less puffy than murmura but has a similar flavor.

Directions:

1. Preheat oven to 200 degrees. Spread the murmura in a baking dish and toast in the oven for 20 minutes, stirring halfway through. The murmura should just be starting to turn golden brown. Carefully pour into a large bowl and set aside to cool. (Skip this step if using crisped rice cereal).

2. Meanwhile, spread the chickpeas out on a clean paper towel and pat dry.

3. Raise the oven temperature to 350 degrees. Toast the almonds in the baking dish for 5 minutes. Add to bowl with murmura.

4. Raise the oven temperature to 425 degrees. Add the chickpeas to the baking dish and bake for 20 minutes, until they are just starting to get crispy. For crispier chickpeas, bake for 30 minutes, watching carefully to make sure they do not burn.

5. Add the chickpeas to the bowl, along with the raisins, coconut, sugar, and salt. Stir thoroughly.

6. Enjoy as a snack! Today people in India like to have this snack with a cup of tea.

Lord Kubera and Ganesha

Lord Kubera, the Hindu god of wealth, decided to display his riches by putting on a feast for the other gods and goddesses. He sent invitations to every deity he could think of. But sending an invitation to Lord Shiva would not be enough. Lord Shiva was the most powerful of the gods. His consort, Parvati, was the goddess of power. No, a simple invitation brought by messenger would not do. Lord Kubera traveled to their home in Mount Kailash himself.

To Lord Kubera's great disappointment, Lord Shiva and Parvati declined his invitation. His shoulders sagging, Lord Kubera turned to leave. "But," Lord Shiva said, "my son, Ganesha, will attend your feast." Lord Kubera practically skipped down the mountain in his excitement. He barely heard Parvati's warning behind him.

"My son has a voracious appetite. Feed him well!"

On the day of the feast, Lord Kubera made sure everything was perfect. He served the most elegant of foods and displayed all of his riches. The guests came in their finest clothes wearing gold and jewels. Little Ganesha came too. Lord Kubera gave his guests a tour of his home, but Ganesha interrupted him.

"Lord Kubera, I'm hungry!" Lord Kubera smiled at the young god.

"Then let us feast!" Ganesha soon polished off every morsel of food on his plate. And then, to Lord Kubera's horror, Ganesha kept eating. He ate all of the food prepared for the other guests. He ate all of the food saved for the servants. But he was still hungry. "Please," Lord Kubera pleaded, "let me have more food brought to you." Ganesha was too hungry to wait. First, he ate his golden plate and utensils. Then he ate the other dishes and utensils on the table. But he was still hungry. He began chewing on the table itself. Kubera wailed. "Please stop, Lord Ganesha!" Ganesha looked up.

"If you don't give me food, I will eat you!" Lord Kubera and the other guests fled from the palace. Lord Kubera rushed straight back to Mount Kailash to beg for help.

"Your meal was served with pride," Lord Shiva chided Lord Kubera. "You must serve him a meal with love and humility in your heart." Lord Shiva handed Lord Kubera a bowl of puffed rice.

Lord Kubera raced back to his palace, hoping to reach it before Ganesha had eaten the palace itself. He knelt before Ganesha and offered the bowl of puffed rice, filled with love and new humility. Ganesha ate the puffed rice, and at last, was satisfied.

Food in Canaan

Marinated Cucumbers

Phoenician Chickpea Soup

Phoenician Flatbread

Cheese of the Herd

Hummus

Canaan was the ancient region home to the Israelites and the Phoenicians. These cultures shared much in the way of culinary tradition. Later, Hebrew food taboos set the Israelites apart from their neighbors.

The Phoenicians were traders in the Mediterranean trade network. They had many ingredients in common with other cultures in the region. They ate barley and wheat in porridge, bread, and flatbreads. They drank wine and sold it. They ate chickpeas, lentils, and broad beans whole or ground into flour. They used honey and date syrup to sweeten their food. They also ate fruit including figs, pomegranates, and apples. Given their reputation as seafarers, it's not surprising that they also liked fish. They roasted or grilled meat, most often sheep or goat. It's possible they had tasted more exotic items on their trading journeys. The Greek writer, Herodotus wrote about Phoenician travel. He said Phoenician ships had sailed all the way around the continent of Africa. They found the seasons reversed on their southbound journey.

The Phoenicians' neighbors, the Israelites, had a similar diet. The Hebrew Bible, which gives us much of our knowledge about their daily life, lists many foods. From this, we know they ate wheat, barley, figs, pomegranate, olives, and honey.

Archaeology shows they also ate acorns, almonds, and pistachios. They ate sheep, goats, and cattle, but not pork. Dairy products played an important role in the diet. They made soft cheeses like feta and paneer. They used ghee, which is more stable in a warm climate. Their diet was heavily ruled by food restrictions described in their Bible. Observant Jewish people today still observe many of these rules around food. These rules are called "kashrut" or "kosher." People who are kosher do not eat pork or shellfish. They may also follow rules about how animals are slaughtered or prepared. For example, dairy and meat cannot be mixed together or prepared on the same dishes. Orthodox Jews follow kashrut rules strictly. Conservative and Reform Jews may follow some laws or only follow the laws on religious days. Kosher foods are often labeled in modern grocery stores for Jewish customers.

Today's Israeli cuisine is different from Israelite cuisine. Israelis brought Jewish food traditions from all over the world with them. These traditions combined with the indigenous Palestinian food traditions. Many modern Israeli foods have their roots in Palestinian kitchens.

How do we know? The Hebrew Bible is a written source. The Phoenicians didn't leave behind written records of their food. We know what they traded through their records. We also have the writing of their contemporaries in Greece. Archaeologists have studied remains in the area.

Canaan Menu:

Breakfast:
Milk
Phoenician Flatbread: *p.65*
Puls Punica: *p.19*

Snacks:
Cheese of the Herd: *p.55*
Raisins: *p.41*
Dried apples:*p.42*
Yogurt: *p.58*

Dinner:
Cucumber salad: *p.73*
Phoenician Flatbread: *p.65*
Falafel: *p.86*
Phoenician Chickpea Soup: *p.100*

Dessert:
Fig Cookies: *p.179*
Finikia: *p.177*

Drinks:
Grape Juice: *p.196*

Fruits and Nuts:
Almonds
Apples
Apricots
Dates
Figs
Grapes
Olives
Pistachios
Pomegranates
Quinces
Watermelon

Dairy

Humans domesticated sheep, goats, and cows over 8000 years ago. But why? All adults were lactose intolerant. Lactose intolerance usually begins at around age 3. People likely kept these animals for meat. They may also have kept dairy animals as a backup source of milk for babies. But somewhere along the way, people realized they could eat milk if they turned it into cheese. An old story is that someone discovered cheese by carrying milk in a skin bag. The milk curdled from the enzymes in the skin and the movement of the bag. There is no evidence that this actually happened. It's more likely that people noticed milk curdled in the stomach of young animals butchered for meat. (Animal stomachs contain an enzyme called rennet used to make hard cheeses). Either way, people started making cheese sometime between 6500 and 6000 BCE.

Cheese and butter played an important role in many ancient cultures. The Mesopotamian city of Ur was a center for butter and cheese making. The butter was a clarified butter like today's ghee. The goddess Inanna married her husband Dumuzi for cheese. In Mesopotamia, they ate dozens of kinds of cheese and yogurt. The Egyptians, Israelites, Indus Valley people, Romans, and Persians all ate cheese. In India, they ate soft cheeses like paneer. Because many people in India were vegetarian, they did not use rennet in cheese making. The Israelites ate several kinds of cheese. One was a little like feta cheese. The Greeks and Romans ate soft cheeses like ricotta and hard cheese like pecorino. But as much as the Greeks and Romans loved cheese, they looked down on "butter eaters" from Northern Europe.

MEDITERRANEAN

Cheese of the Herd

The simplest way to make cheese is to heat milk, add an acid, and strain the curds. This type of cheese exists almost everywhere you Ānd dairy animals. In Scotland, it's called crowdie. In India, it's called paneer. In Spanish, it's queso fresco. This type of cheese is even mentioned in early texts such as the Talmud and Bible. It's a mild cheese that goes with almost anything.

GF; V

About ½ pound of cheese

Level of Difficulty: 3

30 minutes

Ingredients:

8 cups (half gallon) whole milk
¼ cup white vinegar
½ teaspoon salt

Special Equipment:
Cheesecloth or butter muslin

Serving tip: This cheese can also be crumbled and used like feta or goat cheese.

Directions:

1. Heat the milk in a saucepan over medium heat, stirring occasionally to avoid burning. When the milk starts to smoke, but before it boils, turn oĀ the heat and immediately stir in vinegar.

2. Let stand 10 minutes.

3. Line a strainer with cheesecloth and place a bowl or pan underneath to catch the liquid (whey).

4. Pour the milk and vinegar mixture through the cheesecloth.

5. Stir the salt into the cheese curds.

6. Let curds stand in a strainer to drain for 1 hour.

7. After the curds have Ānished draining, gather the cheesecloth around the curds and squeeze to remove any additional whey.

8. Transfer the cheese ball to a dish. Cover and refrigerate. Enjoy immediately or refrigerate for up to 3 days.

SCYTHIANS

Quark: Two Ways

Quark is a fermented dairy product popular in Europe even today. It dates back thousands of years. The Scythians made something like quark, which is somewhere between cultured buttermilk and yogurt. It can be used like yogurt in most recipes. You can start with buttermilk from the grocery store or a buttermilk culture.

GF; Vegetarian

4 servings

Level of
Difficulty: 3

1 hour

Ingredients:

1 gallon of milk

1 packet direct set buttermilk starter

OR

2 cups milk

½ cups cultured buttermilk

Ingredients Tip:

Powdered buttermilk cultures are widely available online.

Special Equipment:

Food thermometer
Cheesecloth or butter muslin

Directions:

1. Heat the milk to 88 degrees and remove from heat.

2. Add the packet buttermilk starter and stir thoroughly. If using cultured buttermilk, let the milk cool to room temperature Ārst (70-75 degrees).

3. Cover the pot and let sit at room temperature for 24 hours. It should look as solid as yogurt when it is set.

4. Line a colander with cheesecloth or butter muslin. Pour the curds into the colander.

5. Let the curds drain overnight in the refrigerator.

MESOPOTAMIA, GREECE, ROME, INDIA

Homemade Yogurt

Yogurt was invented sometime about 5000 BC/BCE in Mesopotamia. People likely discovered yogurt by accident when milk fermented naturally. The peoples of ancient Greece and India liked yogurt with honey and so do we!

GF; V

1 quart

Level of
Difficulty: 3

12 hours, including
rest time

Ingredients:

4 cups whole milk

2 tablespoons plain yogurt with live and active cultures (read the label)

Special Equipment:

Thermometer

Directions:

1. In a saucepan, heat the milk to 180 degrees, stirring frequently. Do not boil.

2. Remove the pan from the heat and allow the milk to cool to between 110 and 120 degrees.

3. If a skin has formed on your milk, skim it oÅ Whisk in your yogurt.

4. Pour into a jar or food storage container.

5. Keep warm for at least 6 hours and up to 12 hours.

6. Refrigerate.

Tips:

There are lots of ways to keep the yogurt warm while it's incubating. You can preheat an oven to 170 degrees and then turn it oÅ before putting the container in the oven. You can also wrap the container in towels and put it in a cooler. If you want a thicker yogurt, strain through cheesecloth for 15-30 minutes before refrigerating.

KUSH (ETHIOPIA)

Ayib

Ayib is a soft Ethiopian cheese similar to cottage cheese. It is served with meals to balance out the spiciness of other dishes. You can also just eat it spread on injera *(see p.69)*! This simplified recipe is based on ingredients available during ancient times.

GF; V

4 servings

Level of
Difficulty: 1

5 minutes plus
1 hour rest

Ingredients:

1 cup cottage cheese

1 teaspoon dried parsley

1 teaspoon lemon juice

¼ teaspoon ground black pepper

Ingredients tip:
You can also use the Cheese of the Herd on page53. Strain for 15-30 minutes instead of an hour, until there is no clear whey visible but the cheese is still Āuid and easy to stir. Add the rest of the ingredients from this recipe.

Directions:

1. Stir all ingredients together in a bowl.

2. Let rest in the refrigerator for at least one hour.

EAST AFRICA

Sabaayad: Somali Flatbread

While the recipes of Punt are as lost as its borders, flatbreads have been fairly universal throughout human history. This particular flatbread is traditional in Somalia today and may have its roots in the kitchens of that ancient kingdom.

V+ variation, DF

4 servings

Level of Di~culty: 1

5 minutes plus 1 hour rest

Ingredients:

2 cups all-purpose flour (240g) plus more for dusting
1 cup whole wheat flour (120 g)
½ teaspoon salt
2 tablespoons ghee or olive oil, plus more for cooking
1 cup water

Directions:

1. Whisk together the flour, whole wheat flour, and salt.

2. Stir in the ghee or oil and mix thoroughly.

3. Pour in the water, stirring as you go.

4. When the mixture starts to pull together, knead it with your hands in the bowl. To knead the dough, roll it into a ball, press it flat, and fold it in half. Repeat until the dough is smooth and stretchy.

5. Let rest for 30 minutes.

6. Divide the dough into eight equal portions and roll each piece into a ball.

7. Lightly flour a surface and use your hands to press the balls into discs about the thickness of a pancake. Brush about a teaspoon of oil or ghee on both sides of each disc.

8. Heat a skillet on medium heat and add one disc. Cook for about a minute, until it is browned. Then flip and continue cooking until the second side is browned.

9. Repeat for the remaining pieces and serve hot.

AFRICA, EUROPE, ASIA, AUSTRALIA

Millet Flatbread

GF, DF, V, V+

Millet was a common ingredient in flatbreads everywhere that it grew. The most simple flatbreads were just water and ground millet cooked on top of hot stones. You might have found it prepared this way in Jomon Japan or ancient Australia. It's still made today in India where it is called Bajri no Rotlo. We have modified the recipe quite a bit for modern American tastes, but millet flour has a strong flavor of its own. The modern addition of baking soda helps to improve the texture of the bread, but could be omitted for authenticity. This flatbread goes well with soups and saucy dishes. You can also serve it warm, topped with butter and honey.

6 flatbreads

Level of Difficulty: 3

10 minutes

Ingredients:

2 cups (280g) millet flour

¼ teaspoon salt

¼ teaspoon baking soda

2 ½ cups boiling water 2 tablespoons honey (use vegan honey if desired)

Cooking oil

Ingredients Tip:
You can order millet flour on-line.

Directions:

1. Stir together the millet flour, salt, and baking soda.

2. Combine the boiling water and honey and stir thoroughly.

3. Stir the honey-water into the dry ingredients and combine thoroughly. It should resemble pancake batter

4. Let the batter rest for 15 minutes to give the millet time to absorb the water.

5. Heat up a cast iron or nonstick skillet on medium heat. Add a small amount of the cooking oil of your choice, just enough to coat the surface.

6. Add the batter using a ¼ cup scoop. Pour slowly and cook 3 minutes per side, flipping when it starts looking dry around the edges.

7. Serve warm.

DeÁnition

Proof: ProoÁng yeast in water gives it a chance to prove it's still alive. It's giving the yeast a chance to eat some sugar and get a head start. It's especially important for drier bread dough. Anytime you let the yeast hang out and ferment, it's called prooÁng. This bread dough is proofed twice, in addition to prooÁng the yeast.

EGYPT

Egyptian Barley Bread

Barley was a major crop in ancient Egypt. They used barley for beer, bread, and porridge. Beer and bread both began with the use of wild-occurring yeasts, but eventually the ancient Egyptians learned to purposefully culture yeast. Today, archaeologists have even recreated ancient Egyptian bread using the original yeasts. The yeasts lay dormant for thousands of years but were then ready to get back to work making delicious bread.

Vegetarian, DF

4 servings

Level of Difficulty: 3

1 hour

Ingredients:

½ cup warm water (about 100 degrees)

2 tablespoons honey

2 ¼ teaspoons instant yeast

½ teaspoon salt

2 eggs, lightly beaten

2 tablespoons olive oil

2 cups (320g) barley flour + more for dusting

Special Equipment:
Thermometer*

Ingredients Tip: Barley flour can be ordered online

*If you don't have a thermometer, try this: put your wrist under running water for 15 seconds. If it feels warm but not hot, that's about 100 degrees and good enough for your yeast!

Kneading tip: Use a rimmed baking sheet lined with a silicone mat or parchment taper for your kneading surface to contain the mess!

Directions:

1. In a large bowl, stir together the warm water and honey. Add the yeast and let it proof for about 5 minutes.

2. Add the salt, eggs, and olive oil and stir.

3. Stir in the flour until the mixture holds together.

4. Dust the work surface with barley flour and dump out the dough.

5. Knead well for 1 minute. The dough will have just slightly more stretch than when you started.

6. Grease a large bowl and put the dough in the bowl. Cover it tightly with plastic wrap.

7. Keep in a warm place (about 75 degrees) for 1 ½ hours. The dough will rise slightly.

8. Turn the dough out on a floured surface and knead again 2 or 3 times.

9. Shape into a round disk. It should be about ½ inch thick.

10. Place in a lightly greased pie pan. Brush the top with olive oil and cut an X across the top, about ½ inch deep.

11. Cover with plastic wrap or a towel and let rise again for 1 hour. The X should look more defined as the dough has expanded.

12. Preheat oven to 425 degrees.

13. Bake for 15 to 20 minutes. The bread is finished when it is pale brown and sounds hollow when tapped.

14. Remove from pan and cool fully on a wire rack before cutting.

MEDITERRANEAN

Phoenician Flatbread

This recipe is for a traditional Lebanese flatbread. Lebanese cooking has its roots in Phoenician food traditions. The baking powder is a modern addition, but a flatbread like this could easily have been made during ancient times. This is an appropriate flatbread to serve with any of the Mediterranean recipes.

GF variation; V

4 large flatbreads

Level of Difficulty: 3

15 minutes

Ingredients:

2 cups flour (260g) + additional for dusting

2 teaspoons baking powder

½ teaspoon salt

2 cups full-fat Greek yogurt

Directions:

1. Stir together all the dry ingredients.

2. Stir in 1 ½ cups yogurt until a dough forms. If the mixture is crumbly, add additional yogurt one tablespoon at a time until the mixture holds together.

3. Turn out your dough onto a lightly floured surface and use your hands to flatten it into a roughly 8 inch circle.

4. Break it into quarters, flattening each quarter to about ¼ inch thick.

5. Heat a nonstick pan over medium heat.

6. Cook each flatbread until well browned on each side, about 7 minutes per side.

7. Serve with soup, cheese, or honey.

Gluten Free Variation:

Substitute gluten free flour for the wheat flour.

MESOAMERICA

Tortillas

The oldest corn tortillas in the world are over 10,000 years old, so it's a safe bet to use them for any Mesoamerican culture. Today, many cooks prefer to use a tortilla press but they were traditionally flattened between the hands. It takes a lot of practice to make a thin tortilla, but thicker ones still make delicious tacos. While you can use a spoon to stir, it's a lot of fun and more traditional to stir it with your bare hands!

GF; DF; V; V+

16 tortillas

Level of
Difficulty: 3

30 minutes

Ingredients:

2 cups (280g) masa harina
2 cups water, more or less as needed

Special Equipment:
Tortilla Press (optional)

If you have a tortilla press:
Place a ball of dough between two sheets of plastic wrap. Press until the tortillas are 5 inches in diameter.

TIP: Throughout the process, hands should be rinsed of the sticky dough and fingers kept wet to more easily form the dough.

Directions:

1. Pour the masa into a large bowl and add about 1 ½ cups of cold water.

2. Stir well. Add additional water, a few tablespoons at a time, until the mixture resembles wet clay.

3. Divide the dough into balls roughly 2 inches across and weighing about 55 grams.

4. Cover the dough balls with a wet paper towel.

5. Heat a skillet on medium heat.

6. Take one ball at a time and flatten it by flipping it back and forth between your flattened fingers, rotating it at the same time.

7. Put the tortilla in the pan and cook until starting to brown on the bottom, about a minute. Then flip and cook on the other side. Turn down the heat if needed to keep the tortillas from burning. If they are thick, they will take longer to cook

8. Keep warm under a clean towel until ready to serve.

KUSH (ETHIOPIA)

Easy Injera

Injera is the iconic flatbread of Ethiopia. Traditional injera uses a starter, similar to sourdough. It takes over a week to develop the starter. After preparing the batter, it is poured onto a large specialized pan in a perfect spiral. The rest of the meal is served on top of the injera, with small pieces used as utensils to scoop up the food. Real injera has a delightful sour taste. It is soft, spongy, and pliable. Pouring injera in a perfect spiral is a true art. This version is milder and a little easier to make. You can skip the overnight rest if necessary, but it makes it taste better! (Photo of Easy Injera on p.53)

GF, DF; V; V+

4 servings

Level of Difficulty: 3

30 minutes

Ingredients:

1 ½ cups (280g) teﬀ ﬂour
2 cups water
1 ½ teaspoons baking powder
¼ teaspoon salt
Vegetable oil

Ingredients Tip:

Teﬀ ﬂour is available in African markets or online

Directions:

1. Stir the ﬂour and water together well. Cover with a dish towel and let sit overnight.

2. Stir the baking powder and salt into the batter. If the batter isn't runny, add ¼ cup of water at a time until it is like runny pancake batter.

3. Heat a nonstick or cast iron skillet on medium heat. Add just enough oil to coat the surface.

4. Pour ¼ cup of batter slowly into the pan. You can use more batter to make larger injera, but they are harder to ﬂip.

5. Cook until there are bubbles and the top is starting to turn dull, about 1 ½ minutes.

6. Add a lid (glass is best!) and cook until the edges start to curl up, about another 1 ½ minutes.

7. Run a spatula under the entire injera to loosen it then carefully transfer it to a plate.

8. Repeat until you have used all the batter and cover until ready to serve.

Dried Spiced Beef

In the days before refrigeration, drying was one way to preserve meat. Egyptian tombs have images of meat drying, but this is a technique that was practiced all over the world. Today, oven-drying or using a dehydrator is a more reliable method. By using fajita meat, there is no need for knife work in this recipe.

GF; DF

About 16 strips

Level of
Difficulty: 2

2-3 hours

Ingredients:

1 lb pre-sliced beef packaged for fajitas or stir fry

1 teaspoon salt

½ teaspoon ground coriander

¼ teaspoon ground mustard

¼ teaspoon ground cumin

½ teaspoon liquid smoke (optional)

Special Equipment:
Oven-safe wire racks

Directions:

1. Preheat the oven to 170 degrees.

2. Stir together the spices in a small bowl.

3. Toss together the meat strips, spices, and liquid smoke if using.

4. Place wire racks on the top of rimmed baking sheets.

5. Spread the strips on the top of the baking sheets so that they are not touching.

6. Bake for 2-3 hours, checking for doneness every thirty minutes after the 2 hour mark.

7. Refrigerate for up to a week.

VEGETABLES
AND
SIDE DISHES

MEDITERRANEAN

Cucumber Salad

Marinated cucumbers were popular throughout the Mediterranean in ancient times. Cucumbers of the time period were bitter and difficult to digest unless they were marinated or pickled.

GF; DF; V; V+

4 servings

Level of Difficulty: 2

30 minutes

Ingredients:

4 cucumbers

1 tablespoon kosher salt

½ cup red wine vinegar

1 tablespoon honey

½ teaspoon onion powder

⅛ teaspoon ground black pepper

.

Directions:

1. Peel the cucumbers. Then cut them in half and use a spoon to scrape out and discard the seeds.

2. Slice the cucumbers thinly. Put them in a colander and toss with the salt.

3. Let the cucumbers drain in the colander for 30 minutes to an hour.

4. Rinse the cucumbers thoroughly and dry on paper towels.

5. In a small bowl, mix together the wine vinegar, honey, onion powder, and ground pepper.

6. Put the cucumbers in a serving bowl and toss with the dressing.

7. Let rest for at least 30 minutes for the cucumbers to absorb the dressing.

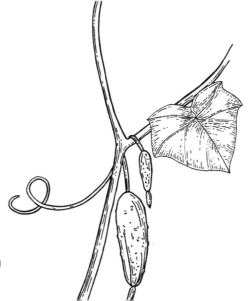

Food in
Ancient North America

The continent of North America is over 9 million square miles. It has deserts, mountains, rainforests, and tundra. It includes Canada, Mexico, the United States, and the countries of Central America. Although a trade network connected many cultures in ancient North America, the availability of food items depended on the region.

The northeastern part of the continent is the only place to grow sugar maple trees. It was labor intensive to boil down maple sap into a delicious syrup or even crystallized sugar. But it then kept for a long time. We don't know exactly when Indigenous peoples started boiling down maple sap to make syrup, only that it was already an old practice by the time Europeans colonized the Americas. The Menominee, Haudenosaunee (Iroquois), and Anishinaabe (Ojibwe) peoples all have maple syrup traditions. They each have their own traditional story about its invention (see p.26) The northeast is also the only place where cranberries grow. The Omàmiwinini (Algonquin) and Wampanoag peoples use cranberries for food, medicine, and dye.

Corn wasn't present in most of North America until thousands of years after it was domesticated in Mexico. It didn't arrive in the Midwest until about 1000 AD/CE. With corn came the agricultural technique known as the Three Sisters Garden. Wild rice grew in the Great Lakes region, where people gathered it by canoeing into the stands of tall grass. Even today, the Anishinaabe and Neshnabé (Patawatomi) peoples consider wild rice a sacred food. In the Southwest, blue corn grew better than the yellow variety. It was an important part of the diet of the Ancestral Puebloans. Pine nuts and sunflower seeds nourished the people in the Four Corners area. This is now Colorado, Utah, New Mexico, and Arizona.

On the West Coast, ancient fishers caught salmon and halibut for their tables. The people of California gathered acorns and continue to do so today. People all over the continent hunted big game like deer, bison, elk, or moose. Generally, Native Americans did not use salt in their cooking, although it was available in coastal areas. Most cultures obtained food through hunting, fishing, farming, and gathering. Boiling, roasting, and drying were all common techniques. Northeastern nations dug pits to cook their feasts of clams and oysters. This is the ancestor of today's New England clam bakes.

In pre-European contact times, a vast trade network connected many of these cultures. European colonization drastically changed the food landscape. White settlers pushed Native peoples off ancestral lands. These Native peoples lost their traditional foods as well as their homes. The United States government encouraged the extermination of American bison. By killing the bison, they deprived Native peoples of a major food source and destroyed their way of life. In modern times, fry bread is a staple at powwows, but it is a direct result of forced marches and rationing.

Today, Native people are working to reclaim their food heritage. Chefs like Sean Sherman (The Sioux Chef) use traditional ingredients to create new and exciting meals. Members of the Eastern Band of Cherokee Indians successfully obtained permits to gather sochan from Smoky Mountain National Park. Sochan is a type of coneflower and a traditional food for the Cherokee. Kanien'kehá ka (Mohawk) chef Dave Smoke McCluskey of Corn Mafia produces grits and masa using traditional methods.

Other options: Visit a Powwow or Native American cultural center. If you have a Native American cultural center nearby, see if they offer courses or information. Look for cookbooks written by the members of the nations from your area. Take a foraging class and learn about the native plants where you live. Always make sure you know what you are eating and follow the rules for gathering wild foods.

Ancient North America Menu:

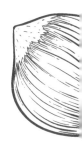

Breakfast:
Acorn Cakes: *p.25*

Snack:
Popcorn: *p.43*

Dinner:
Puebloan Beans and Hominy: *p.115*
Puebloan Hearty Soup: *p.121*

Drinks:
Mint Tea: *p.207*

Fruits and Nuts:
Acorns *(White Oak only for raw eating)*
Blackberries
Blueberries
Cherries
Cranberries
Currants
Grapes
Hazelnuts
Hickory
Plums
Strawberries
Sun
ower Seeds
Walnuts

75

Maize and Squash Salad

During pre-Hispanic times, Mesoamericans did not use cooking oils. Their main techniques were roasting and boiling. Here we use a skillet instead of roasting. This salad makes a great side dish or taco topping.

GF; DF; V; V+

4-6 servings

Level of Difficulty: 3

15 minutes

Ingredients:

1 tablespoon vegetable oil

1 zucchini, chopped

1 pound of frozen corn

1 teaspoon salt

½ cup cilantro, minced

½ cup chopped tomato

Directions:

1. In a skillet, heat the vegetable oil on medium high heat until shimmering.

2. Add the zucchini and cook, stirring frequently, until it just starts to brown.

3. Add the frozen corn and salt, and continue to cook, stirring frequently, until the vegetables are all hot and any water has evaporated from the pan.

4. Remove from heat and stir in the cilantro and tomato. Serve warm, room temperature, or cold.

Peruvian Lima Bean Salad:
Ensalada de Pallaras

Indigenous Peruvians began cultivating lima beans between 6000 and 5000 BC/BCE. This staple food quickly gained in popularity when the Spanish took it back to Europe. European Slavers used it on their ships, introducing the crop to Africa. George Washington and Thomas JeÃerson had it in their gardens. Today it is part of that very southern dish, succotash. This dish is a traditional Peruvian salad symbolic of the Columbian exchange that came thousands of years after the Chavin cooked their lima beans. Cabbage, onions, and limes all have Asian origins while oregano and olive oil came from the Mediterranean. The lima beans, tomatoes, and peppers are all related to native Peruvian crops.

GF; DF; V; V+

4 servings

Level of
Difficulty: 2

45 minutes

Ingredients:

1 lb frozen lima beans

½ pound thinly sliced red or green cabbage

1 cup chopped tomatoes

1 red bell pepper, chopped

½ cup chopped red onion

2 radishes, minced

¼ cup lime juice

1 tablespoon red wine vinegar

1 teaspoon dried oregano

¼ teaspoon salt

¼ teaspoon ground black pepper

2 tablespoons olive oil

Directions:

1. Put the lima beans in a microwave safe bowl with 2 tablespoons of water. Microwave for 6 minutes, stirring halfway through. Let cool.

2. Combine lima beans, cabbage, tomatoes, bell pepper, onions, and radishes in a large bowl.

3. Whisk together the lime juice, vinegar, oregano, salt, and pepper in a small bowl. Whisking constantly, pour in the olive oil in a slow stream.

4. Toss the vegetables with the dressing and let sit for 30 minutes to an hour in the refrigerator before serving to let the Āavors meld.

Cowpeas and Plantains

Cowpeas have been cooked in West Africa for thousands of years. They are related to the black-eyed pea, a popular staple in southern cooking. Africans brought their cooking traditions with them to the Americas during the slave trade, adapting to ingredients that were available. Originally, the people of the Ghana Empire would have used a diﬀerent green similar to spinach.

GF; DF; V; V+

6 servings

Level of Difficulty: 3

45 minutes

Ingredients:

2 cups vegetable broth

2 cans black-eyed peas or cowpeas, rinsed and drained

1 ripe yellow plantain, peeled and sliced into ¼ inch slices

2 cups tightly packed spinach, roughly chopped

1 teaspoon salt

Ingredients Tip:
Ripe plantains have many dark spots or are even all black. They should still be ﬁrm to the touch. To peel plantains, use a sharp knife to cut down the entire length of the peel. Instead of peeling top to bottom like a banana, peel by pulling the strips from side to side.

Directions:

1. Add the broth and peas to a medium pot and bring to a boil on high.

2. Reduce heat to a simmer and add the plantains.

3. Simmer for 30 minutes.

4. Stir in the spinach and salt and cook for another 5 minutes.

5. Serve over rice or alone.

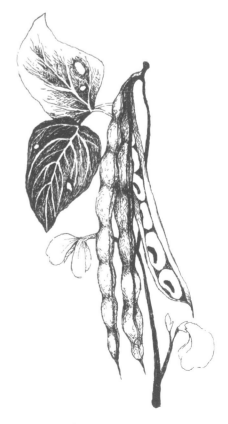

Marinated Beets

Beets were a popular vegetable in ancient Greece and were often served at the beginning of the meal to increase appetite.

GF; DF; V; V+

4 servings

Level of
Difficulty: 3

1 to 1 ½ hours

Ingredients:

1 bunch beets

1 tablespoon red wine vinegar

2 tablespoons olive oil

1 teaspoon salt

½ teaspoon ground coriander

½ teaspoon garlic powder

⅛ teaspoon ground black pepper

Ingredients Tip:
You can use the greens leftover from this recipe to make Apicius' Vegetable Soup on pg.110.

Directions:

1. Trim the greens oﬀ the beets if necessary and wash the beets.

2. Put the beets in a pot and cover with an inch of water.

3. Bring to a boil then reduce to a simmer and cover.

4. Simmer for 45 minutes to an hour, or until a fork pierces the largest beet easily.

5. Meanwhile, whisk together the rest of the ingredients.

6. Use a slotted spoon to put the hot beets into a bowl of cold water.

7. Let rest for about ten minutes, until the beets are cool enough to handle. The skins should slide right oﬀ *(If you do it directly in the water, there will be less mess from the beet juice).*

8. Cut the beets in half and then into ½ inch slices.

9. Toss the beets with the dressing and serve warm or at room temperature.

Food in Ancient
Mesopotamia

Mersu

Babylonian Lamb Stew

Hen with Herbs

Babylonian Turnips

Sumerian Lentil Stew

Mesopotamia means "The Land Between Two Rivers." It is the region between the Tigris and Euphrates Rivers in an area called the Fertile Crescent. Today, the same region includes parts of Iraq, Kuwait, Syria, Turkey, and Iran. Mesopotamia was home to some of the world's earliest cities, like Uruk and Babylon. The oldest known cookbooks in the world come from Babylon. Ancient cooks carved their recipes onto clay tablets. Imagine their surprise if they knew people were cooking their recipes thousands of years later! The tablets date from around 1600 BC/BCE.

Mesopotamia means "The Land Between Two Rivers." It is the region between the Tigris and Euphrates Rivers in an area called the Fertile Crescent. Today, the same region includes parts of Iraq, Kuwait, Syria, Turkey, and Iran. Mesopotamia was home to some of the world's earliest cities, like Uruk and Babylon. The oldest known cookbooks in the world come from Babylon. Ancient cooks carved their recipes onto clay tablets. Imagine their surprise if they knew people were cooking their recipes thousands of years later! The tablets date from around 1600 BC/BCE.

Meals played a central role in Mesopotamian society. Religious rituals included "godly meals," food prepared as offerings in temples. The goddess Inanna required daily offerings of cheese and butter. Each temple had its own brewers, bakers, and cooks. When the offering was complete, priests gave away the food. All formal agreements were sealed with a meal. Kings threw lavish feasts to welcome important people to their court. "Amelu sa tabtiya" was Assyrian for "man of my salt", which meant a friend.

What did they eat? They grilled and stewed meats, serving them with flat breads and vegetables. They ate fruits and pastries sweetened with honey. Cheese and butter rounded out the diet. There were dozens of kinds of cheese, from hard cheeses to soft cheeses and yogurts. Wine and beer accompanied every meal. Most Mesopotamians ate two meals per day. They ate once in the morning and once in the evening. They had a basic recipe for preparing meat: boil water and add meat, leeks, garlic, fats, and salt.

How do we know what they ate? Clay tablets give us recipes, food inventories, and lists of grave goods. The Epic of Gilgamesh describes food-based events like eating at an inn.

Ancient Mesopotamia Menu:

Breakfast
Barley Porridge: *p.14*
Date Syrup and Date Paste *p.221*

Snack:
Yogurt: *p.58*
Raisins: *p.41*
Dried apples: *p.42*
Barley Bread *p.63*

Dinner:
Babylonian Turnips: *p.85*
Sumerian Lentil Stew: *p.101*
Babylonian Hen: *p.154*
Babylonian Lamb Stew: *p.147*

Dessert:
Mersu *p.175*

Drinks:
Grape Juice *p.196*

Fruits and Nuts:

Almonds
Apples
Apricots
Dates
Figs
Grapes
Melons
Pears
Pistachios
Plums
Pomegranates
Walnuts

Babylonian Turnips

Today, Babylon's famous clay tablets are owned by Yale University. Scholars refer to them as the Yale Tablets. This one is from Yale Tablet 25--recipe XXV. The original recipe calls for blood and flour, but we have adapted it for modern tastes.

"Turnips with herbs – Ingredients and method: Prepare water, add fat, turnips. Add a chopped mix of shallots, arugula, and coriander that have been mixed with semolina or other flour and moistened with blood. Cook until done. Add mashed leeks and garlic." --Credit to Silk Road Gourmet for the translation.

GF; DF; V; V+

4 servings

Level of Difficulty: 3

30 minutes

Ingredients:

1 tablespoon olive oil

1 shallot, peeled and minced

1 leek, cleaned and sliced thinly

2 cloves garlic, peeled and minced *(about 2 teaspoons)*

1 pound turnips, peeled and chopped into 1-inch pieces

1 bunch cilantro, minced *(about ¼ cup)*

Directions:

1. Heat the olive oil in a medium pot until shimmering.

2. Saute the shallot, leek, and garlic until soft.

3. Add the turnips and cover with water by about an inch.

4. Bring to a boil, then cover and reduce to a simmer.

5. Simmer for about 25 minutes until the turnips are soft but not mushy.

6. Strain the turnips and stir in the cilantro.

Falafel

GF; DF; V; V+

16 Patties

Level of
Difficulty: 3

24 hours soak
+ 45 minutes

Believe it or not, falafel is a food surrounded by controversy. All of its ingredients were available to the Israelites, and some people speculate that chickpea patties have been part of the diet for thousands of years. They may even have been part of an ancient Egyptian breakfast. It's possible, but the modern falafel was invented by Copts. The Copts were Egyptian Christians. In Egypt, falafel is made with fava beans. Its popularity spread throughout the Middle East, including to Palestine. However, after the modern nation of Israel was founded in 1948, its Jewish citizens wished to connect with their ancient heritage. They learned to make falafel from Palestinian restauranteurs. Over time, falafel became the national snack of Israel. Because of political tension between Palestinians and Israelis, the debate about falafel's origins has its roots in national identity.

Ingredients:

1 pound dried chickpeas

6 scallions, chopped

3 cloves garlic, peeled (about 1 tablespoon minced)

1 cup parsley, roughly chopped

2 teaspoons ground cumin

1 teaspoon kosher salt

¼ teaspoon ground black pepper

Olive oil

Ingredients Tip:
You must use dried chickpeas rather than canned for this recipe to get falafel's signature crunch. Canned chickpeas will result in a softer patty.

Special Equipment:
Food processor

Directions:

1. Cover the chickpeas with cold water and stir in a tablespoon of salt. Let sit for 24 hours.

2. Preheat oven to 375 degrees.

3. Drain the chickpeas and rinse thoroughly.

4. Add the chickpeas to a food processor with the remaining ingredients. Process for 1 minute, stopping to scrape the sides if necessary.

5. Grease a ¼ cup measure and a baking sheet with olive oil. Use the cup to scoop up the mixture.

6. Form into patties about ½ inch thick on the baking sheet.

7. Bake for about 25 minutes, flipping them over halfway through.

8. Serve with yogurt for dipping.

Food in
Ancient Peru

Peruvian Lima
Bean Salad

Quinoa Stew

Olluquito Con
Charqui

Chili Pastes

The Chavin Culture of Peru existed from 900 BC/BCE to 200 BC/BCE. The Inca Empire came much later, founded in 1438 AD/CE. The Incans descended from a tribe dating back to the 12th century. Before the Inca ruled, the Tiwanaku and Wari Empires held sway in the Andes Mountains. But there is something special about the cultures of the Andes. Scholars describe the civilization as "pristine," or not influenced by other cultures. We can combine archaeology and Spanish writing about the Incas to paint a picture of food in the ancient Andes.

Around 5600 BC/BCE, the people of the Andes domesticated peanuts. They ate them roasted in the shell, just like we do today, or ground them into peanut butter. Potatoes are even older, dating back to 8000

BC/BCE. They roasted them or stuck them in stews. They also developed an early technique for freeze-drying potatoes. There were endless varieties. Even today, around 4,000 types of potato grow in Peru. They raised llamas and alpacas for meat, wool, and as pack animals. They also raised guinea pigs for meat. The Incas roasted them by stuffing them with hot stones and herbs. In their gardens, they grew tomatoes, squash, kidney and lima beans, sweet potatoes, and chili peppers. Quinoa and maize were both used to make drinks, stews, and breads.

The Inca also ate insects including mayfly larvae, caterpillars, beetles, and ants. They caught fish, which were often dried and stored. They hunted deer and frogs. They collected algae from rivers and seaweed from the coast. The variety of food seems endless. Do you like avocados, dragonfruit, or passionfruit? You could find all of them in ancient Peru. Then there are tubers, herbs, and fruits known only by their Quechua names. Quechua is the Incan language. The Spanish observed that no one in the Incan Empire ever went hungry. Food was abundant, managed by the leaders, and communal. We don't know how much of the Incan food tradition came from earlier Andean cultures. But it's clear that there were many good things to eat even in the often harsh climate of the Andes.

How do we know? Many people living in the Andes today continue the culinary traditions of their ancestors. The Spanish wrote about Andean food when they colonized the area.

Ancient Peru Menu:

Breakfast:
Quinoa: *p.89*

Snack:
Popcorn: *p.43*
Peanut Butter: *p.223*

Dinner:
Peruvian Lima Bean Salad: *p.79*
Quinoa Stew: *p.102*
Olluquito Con Charqui: *p.111*

Dessert:
Mazamorra Morada: *p.161*

Drink:
Chicha Morada: *p.201*

Fruits and Nuts:
Dragonfruit
Papaya
Passionfruit
Peanuts

PERU

Quinoa

Humans have been growing and eating quinoa (keen-wah) in Peru for thousands of years. They Ārst started raising it to feed their animals about 7000 years ago. By 4000 years ago, this grain-like seed had ended up in their own meals. It's more closely related to spinach than to grains like wheat! The Āavor is fairly plain on its own but it takes toppings well. Try combining it with the chili paste recipes later in this book or just stirring in some butter.

GF; DF; V; V+

3 servings

Level of
Difficulty: 1

10 minutes

Ingredients:

1 cup uncooked quinoa, rinsed thoroughly

2 cups water

1 teaspoon salt

Directions:

1. In a 2 quart microwave-safe container, mix together the quinoa, water, and salt.

2. Microwave for 5 minutes on high then stir.

3. Microwave for 2 minutes and stir again.

4. Microwave for 2 more minutes or until done. The grains should be tender to bite when fully cooked.

Egyptian Lentil Salad

GF; DF; V; V+

The Egyptians didn't leave behind recipes, but they left behind plenty of information about what they ate. Their tombs contained food and their art showed both foods and people cooking. Lentils have been found in some of the oldest tombs, from before there were even pharaohs. We know they grew dill because it was found in the tomb of Amenhotep. This salad can be served hot or at room temperature.

4 servings

Level of
Difficulty: 3

45 minutes

Ingredients:

2 tablespoons olive oil

1 shallot, minced

1 cup lentils, rinsed

2 cups water

½ teaspoon salt

2 tablespoons red wine vinegar

2 tablespoons chopped fresh dill

Directions:

1. Heat the olive oil on medium until shimmering then add the shallot.

2. Cook the shallot for about 5 minutes, until soft.

3. Add the lentils, water, and salt. Bring to a boil then reduce to a simmer.

4. Simmer for about 30 minutes, until the lentils are tender. Stir occasionally, making sure that the lentils don't dry out.

5. If there is any remaining water, drain it oĀ

6. Stir in the vinegar and dill.

Thunder Tea Rice

Before tea became one of the most popular beverages in the world, it was used more in food and medicine. While legends about tea consumption in China place its origins thousands of years in the past, until recently historians thought tea was Ārst consumed during the Han Dynasty (206BCE-220CE, immediately after the Qin Dynasty). Then a discovery in a cave places tea as far back as 2100 BCE. Based on the other substances in the container, historians think that the tea was mixed with other ingredients and consumed as more of a meal. Thunder Tea Rice, or Hakka Lei Cha Rice, is rumored to date back to the Qin Dynasty where it was served to the army. Allegedly, it helped soldiers avoid the plague. This is a simpliĀed version of a dish with many variations. Today, people mix in vegetables, tofu, Āsh, or nuts.

GF; DF; V; V+

6 servings

Level of Difficulty: 3

50 minutes

Ingredients:

2 cups uncooked white rice

4 ½ cups water, divided

1 teaspoon salt, divided

¼ cup packed fresh basil leaves

¼ cup minced cilantro

1 tablespoon toasted sesame seeds

1 tablespoon loose leaf green tea

Optional toppings:
Tofu, green beans

Special Equipment:
Blender

Directions:

1. Rinse the rice thoroughly in a strainer.

2. Bring 4 cups of water to a boil in a medium pot, then add the rice and ½ teaspoon salt. Stir well.

3. Reduce the heat to low and cover, simmering for 20 minutes or until all the water is absorbed.

4. Meanwhile, add ½ cup water, ½ teaspoon salt, and the rest of the ingredients to a blender. Blend until smooth.

5. When the rice is finished, fluff with a fork. Add toppings if desired. Pour the sauce over the rice to serve.

Optional toppings
(Prepare while rice is cooking):

Tofu:
Tofu dates back to the Han dynasty!

Ingredients:
1 package extra Ārm tofu, drained

Directions:

1. Place the tofu on a cutting board lined with a clean towel or paper towels. Place another towel or paper towels on top. Cover with a plate or second cutting board. Weight the top plate down with a heavy cookbook for 30 minutes to press out extra moisture.

2. Slice into ½ inch cubes.

3. Heat cooking oil in a skillet until shimmering.

4. Working in batches if necessary, brown the tofu cubes on all sides.

Green Beans:
Green beans are native to Peru but have a similar Āavor and texture to asparagus beans, which are native to China.

Ingredients:
1 12 ounce package steamable frozen green beans

Directions:
Steam green beans in microwave according to package directions.

INDIA

Pulao: Rice Pilaf

GF, DF, V, V+

The history of rice pilaf is a little bit mysterious, but some historians trace the world pilaf back to pulao from India, and that from an old Sanskrit word used in the Mahabharata to describe a mixture of meat and rice. Legend has it that Alexander the Great had this rice dish on his travels in Asia. The oldest written recipe for pilaf comes from a Persian writer in the tenth century but the dish is much older. This vegetarian version is suitable for Ashoka, the Buddhist emperor and would goes well with the proto curry on p.107.

6 servings

Level of Difficulty: Medium

35 minutes

Ingredients:

1 ½ cups basmati rice

3 tablespoons olive oil

¾ teaspoon anise seeds

½ teaspoon ground mace

½ teaspoon caraway seeds

½ teaspoon ground cardamom

½ teaspoon ground ginger

½ teaspoon garlic powder

½ teaspoon ground cinnamon

¼ teaspoon ground cloves

¼ teaspoon nutmeg

1 medium onion, cut in half and thinly sliced

1-2 carrots, peeled and chopped into ¼" cubes, about 1 cup

½ cup frozen peas

3 tablespoons fresh cilantro, stems removed and finely chopped

2 ¾ cups water

1 teaspoon salt

Directions:

1. In a fine mesh strainer, rinse the rice until the water runs clear. Soak the rinsed rice in a bowl of water for at least 15 minutes. Drain.

2. In a medium saucepan, heat the oil on medium until shimmering.

3. Add the spices and cook, stirring constantly, for about 30 seconds.

4. Stir in the onion and cook until golden, stirring regularly.

5. Add carrots, peas, and cilantro. Cook for 3-5 minutes until the carrots begin to soften.

6. Pour in the water and salt and bring to a boil on high heat.

7. Stir in the drained rice and reduce to a simmer.

8. Simmer, covered, for 5 minutes or until all the water is absorbed.

Bariis Xawaash Leb: Turmeric Rice

Rice was domesticated in Asia at least 10,000 years ago and in Africa by 1800 BC/BCE. Today, 3.5 billion people rely on rice as a dietary staple. Turmeric also has its roots in Asia, where it has been cultivated in India for thousands of years. It may not have reached Punt but was used in East Africa by at least 800 AD/CE and is now a common ingredient in Somali dishes.

GF; V

4 servings

Level of Difficulty: 3

30 minutes

Ingredients:

1 tablespoon olive oil

2 tablespoons ghee

1 ½ cups basmati rice, rinsed

½ teaspoon ground turmeric

½ teaspoon ground coriander

½ teaspoon ground cumin

½ teaspoon salt

½ cup loosely packed washed and chopped cilantro, about one bunch

2 ¼ cups water

Directions:

1. Heat the oil and ghee in a saucepan over medium heat, and then add the rice and cook for 2-5 minutes, stirring frequently, until the rice is just starting to brown.

2. Stir in the spices and cook for about 30 seconds, stirring constantly.

3. Add the cilantro and water and bring to a boil.

4. Reduce the heat to a simmer and cook, covered, for about 20 minutes, until the water is fully absorbed.

Gomen: Collard Greens

Collard greens are native to Greece, not Africa. However, sub-Saharan African cultures have a long tradition of cooking greens. Africans brought this tradition to the Americas when they were taken as enslaved people. They also brought their tradition of drinking "pot likker," the nutritious broth made from boiling the leaves in water. Collards are more readily available than native African greens. Today, Ethiopians eat collard greens too. They are called gomen in Amharic, one of Ethiopia's languages.

GF; V

4 servings

Level of
Difficulty: 3

1 hour

Ingredients:

1 pound collard greens, washed

2 tablespoons butter

½ teaspoon paprika

½ teaspoon garlic powder

½ teaspoon salt

Directions:

1. Cut the leaves from the stems of the greens and slice the leaves into 1 inch ribbons.

2. Put into a pot and cover with an inch of water.

3. Bring the water to a boil, then reduce to a simmer for 45 minutes to 1 hour, until the greens are tender.

4. Melt the butter and mix it with the spices.

5. Strain the greens, reserving the pot likker if desired.

6. Stir the spiced butter with the greens, mixing well.

ABORIGINAL AUSTRALIA
"Warrigal" Greens

Many of Australia's native ingredients are not available in American grocery stores. One of the most popular native Australian vegetables is warrigal greens. This leafy green vegetable resembles spinach, so we have used spinach as a substitute in this recipe. We've used a traditional cooking method for vegetables to create this recipe.

GF; DF; V; V+

4 servings

Level of
Difficulty: 3

10 minutes

Ingredients:

1 pound fresh
spinach

1 teaspoon salt

8 cups water

Directions:

1. Wash the spinach thoroughly.

2. Bring the water and salt to a boil in a pot.

3. Stir in the spinach and boil for about a minute.

4. Strain immediately and serve warm.

Serving tip:
Topping the spinach with butter while it is still warm is delicious, if not historically authentic!

Food Taboos

A taboo is "a prohibition imposed by social custom or as a protective measure." (Merriam-Webster dictionary). There are many taboos around food, and few are universal around the world.

In the United States, most people would not consider eating dog or horse. They think nothing of eating hamburgers or hot dogs. Yet in India, cows are sacred, and eating beef is taboo. You might not want to eat insects, but people in Africa, Asia, Australia, and Latin America eat over 1500 species. They are a valuable source of protein, vitamins and minerals. Observant Muslims and Jews avoid pork.

Some food taboos are religious, while others are practical. Sometimes the reasons become mixed. The Hebrew Bible contains many rules about what the Jewish people may and may not eat. These rules are called Kosher. Kosher rules include food taboos and rules about how foods must be prepared. Some historians claim it was a matter of food safety. Other food historians point out that this explanation is incomplete. They say it was about the deeper religious meaning of eating different things. It may also have been a way for the Jewish people to separate themselves from their neighbors.

The Pythagoreans did not eat beans due to their resemblance to embryos. They believed eating beans could interfere with the process of reincarnation. Pythagoras himself died after his refusal to flee across a bean field. They were also vegetarians because of their belief in reincarnation.

Cows are sacred in India because their horns symbolize the gods. Their legs represent the Vedas, sacred religious texts. Many people in India do not eat cows because of this religious symbolism, although they consume dairy products. However, poorer Indians do eat beef because it costs less than other types of meat. Some Hindus and many Buddhists are vegetarians. Buddhists believe that animals can attain enlightenment and therefore should not be killed. Hindu scripture promotes vegetarianism as healthy for the body and spirit. However, about 71 percent of people in India do eat at least some meat.

Sometimes a food taboo helps preserve resources. If multiple groups live in the same region, they may view each other's primary food source as a taboo. Or a taboo might limit the consumption of a scarce food to only one part of the population.

Sometimes foods are perceived as poisonous, even if they are actually edible. Europeans first thought tomatoes were poisonous. Tomatoes are part of the nightshade family. Europe's native nightshades are toxic. Other taboos have their basis in beliefs about health. Papua New Guinea is a place with multiple types of food taboos. The Indigenous people see foods as male or female. Male children must eat male foods to grow up properly. Female children must eat female food for the same reason. Taro is a male food. Sweet potato is a female food. In one area of Papua New Guinea, the chiefs may only eat roasted or fried foods. In Nigeria, parents think coconut milk will stunt their children's intelligence.

These are just a handful of reasons for food taboos. Anthropology professor Thomas J. Barfield described 300 reasons why a food might be taboo in a culture. What foods are taboo in your household?

MAIN COURSES

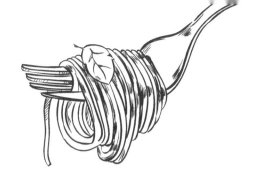

Dinner in the Ancient World

In the days before artificial lighting, people often ate their largest meal in th middle of the day. In English, people named this meal "dinner." It actually comes from a word meaning "breakfast" or the "first big meal of the da ." "Supper" comes from a word meaning "last meal of the day."
In hotter climates, the main meal was always in the evening, when the temperatures are cooler.

The lower classes of each world have always tended to eat vegetables and something made from the staple grain for dinner. The wealthy have always had lavish dinners. In Rome, dinners were three courses. They started with appetizers (gustation). They drank honeyed wine alongside dishes like eggs, snails, oysters, or pickled fish. Then they had the main course (prima mensae). This mea included meat, seafood, vegetables, and porridge. Diners often used bread as a plate or spoon during these courses. Then came dessert (secundae mensae). Dessert usually included fruits and nuts, with honey cakes on fancy occasions. The Greeks also had a three-course meal for dinner. In Ancient Egypt, the wealthy ate three meals a day. Instead of eating midday, they had an evening and a nighttime meal.

Now we usually eat our main meal, or dinner, in the evening. In some parts of the United States, people call that meal "supper" and still call the midday meal "dinner." Whatever you call it, don't call me late!

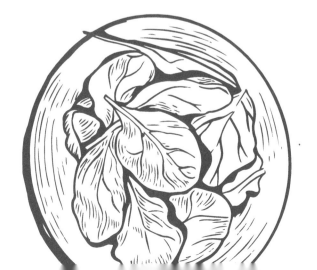

Phoenician Chickpea Soup

Despite having their own writing, no Phoenician recipes have directly survived. This recipe is based on modern Lebanese flavors, traditional cooking methods, and ingredients available to the Phoenicians. Leftover spice mix can be sprinkled on hummus or mixed with olive oil to make a dipping sauce for bread.

GF; DF; V; V+

6 servings

Level of Difficulty: 3

45 minutes

Ingredients:

Phoenician Spice Mix:

1 tablespoon oregano

1 tablespoon cumin

1 tablespoon ground coriander

½ teaspoon salt

Soup:

2 tablespoons olive oil

5 cloves garlic, peeled and minced *(about 2 tablespoons)*

1 tablespoon Phoenician Spice Mix *(above)*

2 15 ounce cans chickpeas, rinsed and drained

4 cups vegetable stock

1 bay leaf

1 tablespoon dried parsley

Directions:

1. Stir all the ingredients for the Phoenician Spice Mix together in a small container.

2. In a saucepan, heat the olive oil on medium until shimmering.

3. Add the garlic and saute until slightly brown, stirring frequently, about five minutes.

4. Add the Phoenician Spice Mix and cook for about 30 seconds, stirring frequently.

5. Add the chickpeas, stock, and bayleaf. Bring to a boil, then reduce to a simmer.

6. Simmer for about 30 minutes, until the chickpeas are tender.

7. Remove from heat and stir in the parsley.

MESOPOTAMIA

Sumerian Lentil Stew

People have been growing lentils in the Fertile Crescent for about 9000 years! Their Latin name is lens culinaris. The modern word "lens" for glasses and contact lenses comes from the double-convex shape of lentil seeds.

GF, DF, V, V+

4 servings

Level of
Difficulty: 3

30 minutes

Ingredients:

2 tablespoons olive oil

1 yellow onion, diced

3 carrots, peeled and diced

3 stalks celery, leaves removed, diced

1 teaspoon minced garlic

½ cup minced cilantro, stems removed

2 cups dry red lentils

6 cups vegetable broth

1 ½ teaspoons cumin

1 tablespoon fresh mint, chopped

1 bay leaf

1 teaspoon salt

¼ teaspoon ground black pepper

2 tablespoons red wine vinegar

Optional:
Sour cream for serving

Directions:

1. In a stock pot, heat the oil over medium heat until it shimmers.

2. Add onion and cook until it starts to turn translucent, about 8 minutes.

3. Add carrots and celery and saute until carrots are softened and the edges of the onion are starting to turn brown.

4. Add garlic and cumin, cooking for another 30 seconds.

5. Stir in lentils and stir to coat.

6. Add broth and bay leaf.

7. Increase heat to high and bring the soup to a boil.

8. Reduce heat to a simmer, then add cilantro and mint. Cover the pot.

9. Simmer for about 30 minutes until the lentils are tender.

10. Remove from heat and stir in red wine vinegar.

11. Serve in bowls and top with sour cream if desired.

Peruvian Quinoa Stew

Pine nuts are native to the Americas, but the onion, garlic, and spices are post-colonization Āavorings in this modern traditional Peruvian dish.

GF; DF; V; V+ | 4 servings | Level of Difficulty: 3 | 30 minutes

Ingredients:

1 tablespoon cooking oil

1 medium onion, peeled and diced

1 clove garlic, minced (about 1 teaspoon)

1 teaspoon salt

1 teaspoon cumin

1 teaspoon oregano

4 cups vegetable broth

1 cup quinoa, rinsed thoroughly

1 teaspoon amarillo paste *(recipe on pg.225)*

4 ounces pine nuts, toasted

¼ cup parsley, chopped Āne

Ingredients Tip:
Amarillo paste is also available at international markets. Look for a yellow paste in a jar near other Peruvian ingredients.

Directions:

1. Heat the oil in a pot on medium heat and add the onion. Saute for about 5 minutes, until the onion is soft.

2. Add the garlic and spices and cook for 30 seconds.

3. Add the vegetable broth, quinoa, and amarillo paste.

4. Bring to a boil then reduce to a simmer and cook for about 15-20 minutes, until the mixture is thick and quinoa is tender.

5. Serve topped with pine nuts and parsley.

INDIA

Mauryan Empire Chana Dal

GF; DF; V; V+

This dish was allegedly prepared at Chandragupta Maurya's wedding feast. Unlike many royal marriages, this was one based on love. Chandragupta Maurya fell in love with a Greek princess named Helen and married her against her parent's wishes. Chandragupta had defeated her father in a war. Perhaps he was still upset! People in India still make dal, a lentil stew.

4 servings

Level of Difficulty: 3

45 minutes

Ingredients:

1 tablespoon ghee or olive oil

1 onion, diced

1 inch fresh ginger, peeled and grated

2 teaspoon ground coriander

2 teaspoon ground cumin

1 teaspoon salt

¼ teaspoon ground cardamom

¼ teaspoon turmeric

2 cans chickpeas, drained and rinsed

1 cup red lentils, rinsed

3 cups vegetable broth

Optional:
Top with plain yogurt.

Directions:

1. In a medium pot, heat the oil on medium heat and add the onion. Saute until soft and translucent, about 5 minutes.

2. Add the spices and cook for about 30 seconds.

3. Add the chickpeas, lentils, and water. Bring to a boil then reduce to a simmer for about 30 minutes.

4. Serve as is or over cooked rice.

Note: Do not substitute ground ginger for fresh in this recipe.

Food in
Ancient India

Rice Pulao

Proto Curry

Chana Dal

Shrikhand

Shikanji
Nimbu Pani

Murmura
Ladoo

Murmura
Chivda

Do you like spicy food? Indian food today has a reputation for being spicy, but it hasn't always been that way. Chili peppers are native to the Americas. In ancient times, the only peppers available in India were black pepper and long pepper. Long pepper is a spicier relative of black pepper. But that doesn't mean the food was flavorless. There were so many things to eat that the Greeks said no one ever went hungry.

In the cities of the Indus Valley Civilization, they ate mutton, pork, goat, and water buffalo. They raised cattle for beef, and for milk they made into cheese. Archaeologists found perforated pots possibly used in cheese-making. They used milk from water buffalo to drink, and made cheese and yogurt. The river provided fish and shellfish. At first, they ate wild rice, then domesticated rice. It is still an important part of the diet in India today. In the Indus Valley, barley was used more than any other grain. They used it in porridge and bread. Ginger, turmeric, pepper, and cardamom added flavor to a diet of lentils and chickpeas. Fertile soil was perfect for growing many fruits and vegetables. They grew dates, grapes, melons, figs, mango and okra. They also cultivated grains, including wheat and millet. Many people ate a vegetarian diet. The merchants of the Indus Valley traveled to Mesopotamia. They had their own quarters in Mesopotamian cities. Did they exchange food customs in their travels? We can only guess.

People in the Indus Valley used simple cooking techniques. They cooked over a hearth or in a brick fireplace, using clay vessels. In wealthy homes, they also had metal cooking vessels and serving dishes.

The Indus Valley Civilization faded away, but cows moved in. They became a sacred animal early in Indian history. People still ate beef, but more and more Indians became vegetarian. Instead of eating beef, they ate milk products like yogurt and ghee. Pork was no longer popular. In the court of Mauryan King Ashoka, they ate hardly any meat at all. He had converted to Buddhism and vegetarianism. One writer tells us, "Formerly, in the kitchens of the [emperor], several hundred thousand animals were killed daily for food, but now at the time of writing only three are killed-- two peacocks and a deer, though the deer not regularly. Even these animals will not be killed in future." What do you think about those numbers? Do you think they are exaggerating or honest?

Barley was still popular. They made into a pancake called "apupa" which they sweetened with honey. Finally, rice gained popularity in the first millennium BCE. They made porridge, mixed it with vegetables, and ground it into flour. They cooked it with sugar and milk and puffed kernels of rice in hot sand. They sifted the rice out of the sand when it was cooked. The Greeks observed that the people of India ate lots of rice. Alexander the Great brought rice with him on his return journey from India.

The Greeks also wrote about how many fruits and vegetables people in India ate. They had bananas, mango, coconut, dates, pomegranate, grapes, apples, plums, apricots, and citrus fruits. Yum!

In modern India, the cuisine varies from place to place. In general, northern Indian cooking includes naan (a flat bread), meat, and ghee. Southern Indian cuisine has many fresh fruits and vegetables. It is often vegetarian. They use coconut milk instead of cow's milk. All India's major religions have restrictions on eating meat. Hindus don't eat beef because it is sacred. Muslims don't eat pork because

it is unclean. Buddhists are often vegetarian due to their belief in reincarnation. Indian food now incorporates ingredients from the Americas, including tomatoes and chili peppers. Yet the same ancient spices still provide the base of many flavors today.

How do we know what they ate? Archaeologists studied human teeth, animal bones, and preserved remains of food items. They observed foods that grew locally. Then, scientists discovered a new technique. They could extract starch molecules from fifty sources. They studied cooking surfaces, cow teeth, and human teeth. Using this technique, they learned about the ingredients in a "proto curry", like the one you can make in this book. We also know about food from Hindu religious texts. These writings are thousands of years old.

Ancient India Menu:

Breakfast:

Malpua Pancakes: *p.33*

Snacks:

 Murmura Chivda: *p.49*

Yogurt: *p.58*

Cheese of the Herd: *p.55*

Dried Apples: *p.42*

Dinner:

Pulao (Rice Pilaf): *p.92*

Proto Curry: *p.107*

Chana Dal: *p.103*

Dessert:

Shrikhand: *p.189*

Murmura Ladoo: *p163*

Drinks:

Nimbu Pani: *p.197*

Fruits and Nuts:

Bananas

Dates

Grapes

Mangoes

Oranges

Peaches

Plantain

Pomegranates

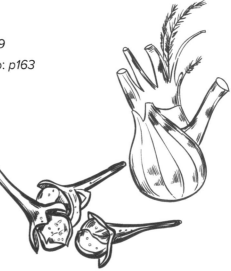

INDIA

Proto Curry

In 2010, archaeologists Arunima Kashyap and Steve Webber analyzed starch molecules from a potsherd to figure out what that pot once held. They found that an ancient cook had used the pot to prepare an ancestor of today's modern curries. The dish included eggplant, salt, ginger, and turmeric. It fits in well with what we know about the diet of the Indus Valley Civilization. Most of the time, people ate a plant-based diet of vegetables, grains, and fruit including dates, grapes, melons, figs, mangos, okra, wheat, and millet. They supplemented this diet with both domesticated animals and hunted game, as well as fish and shellfish from the river. They cooked their meals over a fire in clay pots. Worried about this proto, or first, curry being too spicy? Not yet. Later on, Indians started adding lentils and onions to their curries and spicing them up with white pepper and mustard seed. Hot peppers wouldn't arrive on the scene until after their arrival from the Americas. You can serve this over rice, the classic accompaniment for curry. Experts still debate whether the people of Harappa ate rice or just fed it to their animals. If you do decide to eat it with rice, brown or wild rice would make the most accurate dish.

GF; DF; V; V+

4 servomgs

Level of
Difficulty: 3

50 minutes

Ingredients:

¾ lb eggplants (6 small or 2 large)

1 tablespoon salt

3 tablespoons sesame oil

¼ teaspoon ground turmeric

¼ teaspoon ground cumin

⅛ teaspoon ground ginger

Water

¼ cup cubed fresh or frozen mango

Directions:

1. Peel the eggplant and chop into 1 inch cubes.

2. In a large bowl, toss salt with eggplant and let sit for 30 minutes. Rinse well with cold water.

3. In a skillet, heat the sesame oil on medium high heat until shimmering.

4. Add the spices and cook until they release their aromas, about 60 seconds.

5. Add the eggplant, ¼ teaspoon of salt, and ¼ cup of water. Cover and cook until the eggplant is fork tender, about 10 minutes.

6. Remove lid and add mango.

7. Simmer, uncovered, for 2-3 minutes until the mango is soft.

Looking to make a Mauryan curry instead?

- Use butter or ghee instead of sesame oil (not vegan).

- Chop up an onion and saute it in butter before adding any spices.

- Add lentils with the eggplant and cook until the lentils are tender.

- Stir in ¼ cup of coconut milk or yogurt before serving.

Note: The food writer Soity Banerjee was the first to develop a recipe based on the ingredients of the proto curry. Others have since made their own adaptations.

Food in Ancient Rome

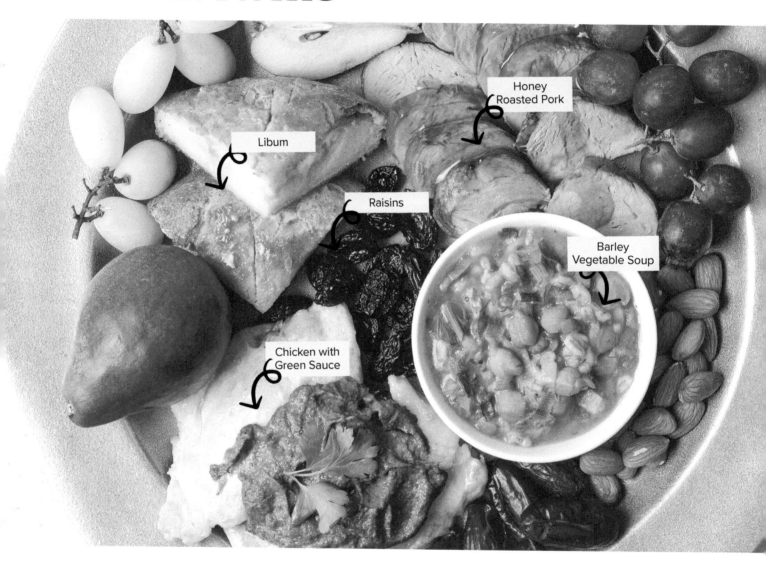

Honey Roasted Pork

Libum

Raisins

Barley Vegetable Soup

Chicken with Green Sauce

When I was a kid, I was fascinated by the lavish banquets of the Ancient Romans. I remember reading about "vomitoria." Supposedly, Romans used these special rooms to throw up after eating too much at a feast. After they emptied their stomachs, they could go back and eat more fancy food. It turns out this is a myth. Vomitoria are actually places where crowds can exit a performance arena at the end of the show.

Historical misunderstandings aside, the ancient Romans loved to eat. They hired cooks and bakers from other countries. Sicilians were the best cooks. Syrians were the best bakers. Everyone ate one meal during the middle of the day. For peasants, it was a simple meal of grains and vegetables. For the rich, it was elaborate feasts of peacocks, dormice, and ostrich brains. The well-trained chefs flavored the food with a heavy hand. Like the Greeks, they enjoyed a combination of sweet and sour flavors. But unlike the Greeks' simple combinations, the Romans used up to 10 different herbs and spices at a time. Fortunately, there is a middle ground with more familiar ingredients. There are many recipes that sound delicious for us today. They made a meat patty of ground pork, pine nuts, salt, and pepper. Sounds tasty!

There were two ingredients that the Romans loved. One was silphium. It's a plant extinct today because the Romans loved it right into extinction. The other is garum, a briny fish sauce. They put garum in almost everything, sweet or savory.

The Romans also loved cheese. They grated hard cheeses like pecorino and sprinkled the grated cheese on their food. They made cheesecakes as offerings to the gods. They made cheese souffles and cheese puddings. Everyone from shepherds to aristocrats ate ricotta cheese. They even imported cheese from the Celts up north!

Fine meals were typically three courses: appetizers, a main course, and dessert. The diners ate with their hands, although they sometimes used bread to scoop up food. They also used spoons for dishes they could not eat by hand. They also sometimes ate off of bread plates. Sometimes dessert was simple: fruit and nuts. Other times, they ate elaborate pastries for dessert.

If you didn't feel like cooking in ancient Rome, you had options. There were plenty of places to eat. There were food stalls around the cities. In Pompeii, archaeologists have discovered 80 thermopolia. A thermopolium is like an ancient fast food counter. The restaurateurs made hot food and then placed the pots in holes in the counter to serve hungry guests. Paintings of animals might have been a picture menu for illiterate diners. One thermopolium served duck, goat, pig, snails, and wine.

What would you order?

How do we know what they ate? The Romans left behind cookbooks. An author using the pen name "Apicius" wrote a cookbook in the 1st century AD/CE. Apicius is one of the most important sources of Roman recipes. Other writers such as Pliny the Elder wrote about food as well as other topics. The eruption of Vesuvius buried the city of Pompeii, preserving restaurants and bakeries.

Ancient Rome Menu:

Breakfast:
Puls Punica: *p.19*

Snacks:
Dried Apples: *p.42*
Raisins: *p.41*
Roasted Chestnuts: *p.47*
Cheese of the Herd: *p.55*

Dinner:
Phoenician Flatbread: *p.65*
Cucumber Salad: *p.73*
Apicius' Vegetable Soup: *p.110*
Split Pea Soup: *p.113*
Chicken with Green Sauce: *p.137*
Honey Roasted Pork: *p.155*

Dessert:
Libum: *p.187*
Honeycomb

Drinks:
Posca: *p.194*
Grape Juice: *p.196*

Fruits and Nuts:
Almonds
Apples
Apricots
Cherries
Dates
Figs
Grapes
Melons
Peaches
Pears
Plums
Pomegranates
Raspberries
Walnuts

WORDS OF WISDOM:
OUR WORD "SOUP" COMES FROM THE LATIN WORD "SUP-PA" WHICH MEANS "SOUP SOAKED IN BROTH." SUPPER COMES FROM THE SAME ROOT!

ROME

Apicius' Vegetable Soup

The Roman cookbook author known as Apicius left behind a cookbook that provides a wealth of information about Roman food. This recipe, like many, calls for the fish sauce named garum. You can substitute modern fish sauce in these recipes. This recipe has been adapted from the original.

DF; GF, V and V+ variation

4 servings

Level of Difficulty: 3

30 minutes

Ingredients:

1 cup dried lentils

1 cup dried chickpeas

1 cup dried split peas

2 tablespoons olive oil

2 leeks, halved and thinly sliced

8 cups vegetable broth

1 cup pearl barley

I bunch beet greens, minced (use beets for marinated beets, p.82)

1 teaspoon ground coriander

1 teaspoon dried dill

1 teaspoon oregano

1 teaspoon fish sauce

Directions:

1. Soak the lentils, chickpeas, and split peas in a bowl of water overnight. Then drain and rinse.

2. Heat the oil in a large pot until shimmering on medium heat. Add the leeks and saute until they are soft.

3. Add the stock, barley, greens, lentils, chickpeas, split peas, and herbs to the pot. Bring to a boil then reduce to a simmer.

4. Simmer for 1 ½ hours, until all the grains and legumes are tender.

5. Add the Āsh sauce and serve.

Gluten Free Variation

Omit the barley and reduce vegetable stock to 5 cups

Vegetarian/Vegan Variation

Substitute soy sauce for the Āsh sauce.

PERU

Olluquito Con Charqi
Potatoes with Jerky

Charqui, or Ch'arki, is a Quechua word for dried meat and gives us our English word "jerky." The Chavin had domesticated llamas for meat and made llama ch'arki for trade. They also ate one of Peru's native tubers, the ulluku or olluco. Both of these ingredients are hard to come by outside of Peru, so we substituted beef jerky and baby potatoes in this modern traditional Peruvian meal. When prepared traditionally, the dish is quite spicy. We have opted to use the chili pastes as a garnish so that each person can control the spiciness of their food. The pastes can be prepared up to a week ahead of time or you can make them while the jerky is soaking and cooking.

DF,GF

4 servings

Level of
Difficulty: 3

30 minutes

Ingredients:

5 oz beef jerky (unflavored), cut into bite-size pieces (look for gluten-free if needed)

4 tablespoons olive or vegetable oil

1 red onion, diced

6 cloves garlic, minced

1 teaspoon ground cumin

1/4 teaspoon ground white pepper

1.5 pounds baby potatoes, thinly sliced

4 cups chicken broth

1 teaspoon salt

Chili Pastes *(see page:225)*

Ingredients Tip:
You can also use the oven-drying technique in Egyptian Spiced Beef (pg. 69) to make your own jerky. Omit the coriander, mustard, and cumin and skip the soaking step in this recipe.

Canned or frozen ollucos are available at some international markets if you prefer to use those instead of baby potatoes. You can also find panca chili paste and amarillo chili paste at these markets.

Directions:

1. Cover the jerky with water and soak for 1 hour.

2. Drain the jerky.

3. In a large saucepan or stock pot, heat 4 tablespoons of oil until shimmering. Add the red onion and cook until it is soft, about 8 minutes.

4. Add garlic, cumin, and white pepper and cook for about 30 seconds.

5. Add jerky and potatoes, then add stock.

6. Bring the mixture to a boil, then reduce heat and simmer for 30 minutes or until potatoes are tender. Add salt if necessary.

7. Serve with chili pastes.

Pisinon Etnos: Split Pea Soup

Legumes such as peas have been growing in the Mediterranean for thousands of years. Pea soup even rated a mention in plays written by Aristophanes. Julius Caesar's wife, Julia, came from the Piso family. The Piso family were named for the humble pea. This soup is simple but delicious, especially when served with pita for dipping. A Greek salad would be nice too, but not very authentic since tomatoes weren't introduced to Greece until the 19th century!

GF, V, DF Variation

4 Servings

Level of Difficulty: 3

75 minutes

Ingredients:

2 tablespoons olive oil

1 onion, chopped

4 cloves garlic, peeled and minced (about one tablespoon)

1 teaspoon salt

⅛ teaspoon ground black pepper

8 cups vegetable or chicken broth

2 cups green split peas, picked through and rinsed

1 lemon, juiced (about 2 tablespoons)

For garnish:

Olive oil

Crumbled feta cheese

Cumin

Paprika

Special Equipment:

Blender or immersion blender

Directions:

1. Heat the olive oil over medium heat until shimmering.

2. Add onions and cook over medium heat until softened, stirring frequently, about eight minutes.

3. Stir in garlic, salt, and pepper, and cook for one to two minutes, stirring constantly to avoid burning the garlic.

4. Pour in broth and peas and bring to a boil.

5. Reduce heat and simmer for 50-60 minutes until the peas are tender.

6. Use an immersion blender to puree the soup until it is almost smooth. If you do not have an immersion blender, carefully transfer the soup to a blender in batches or use a potato masher.

7. Stir in lemon juice and add additional salt and pepper to taste.

8. Ladle into bowls and top each serving with a drizzle of olive oil and a sprinkling of cheese (omit for dairy-free/vegan), cumin, and paprika.

Puebloan Beans and Hominy

The Hopi people are descended from the Ancestral Puebloans and many of their recipes use the same ingredients as their ancestors. Today, the Hopi use dried beans and flint corn to make a stew like this one. They use culinary ash from juniper wood to soak the corn, adding minerals and flavor to make hominy. Pinto beans are widely available, but they would have originally used Anasazi beans *(Anasazi is an older term used to describe the Ancestral Puebloans)*.

GF; DF; V; V+

4 servings

Level of Difficulty: 3

30 minutes

Ingredients:

2 15 ounce cans of pinto beans, drained and rinsed

2 cans of hominy, drained and rinsed

4 cups vegetable broth

1 teaspoon salt (or to taste)

Ingredients Tip:
Using a high quality broth will add flavor to this simple meal. Better Than Bouillon makes an excellent concentrate for broth. It's highly flavorful and very stable in the refrigerator.

Directions:

1. Combine the beans, hominy, and vegetable broth in a medium pot.

2. Bring to a boil then reduce to a simmer for 30 minutes.

3. Taste and add salt if needed (it will depend on your broth).

Japanese Seafood Stew

The Jomon people dined on seafood stews like this one. Shiitake mushrooms are native to Japan. Originally collected by foragers, Japanese people began cultivating shiitake mushrooms at least 2000 years ago. Seaweed has been part of the Japanese diet for at least as long and serves as a source of salt. While the Jomon didn't have scallions, they could have gathered wild onions native to Japan. Today, these ingredients are still popular in Japanese seafood stews.

GF, DF

4 servings

Level of Difficulty: 3

20 minutes

Ingredients:

4 cups water

⅓ cup soy sauce *(gluten-free if necessary)*

¼ cup miso paste

3 tablespoons mirin

4 ounces shiitake mushrooms, rinsed thoroughly

4 scallions, sliced thinly

4 sheets of nori, cut into 1x4 inch strips

½ pound pre-peeled shrimp, tails removed

10 ounces fileted white fish such as cod, tilapia, or grouper, cut into bite-sized pieces

Ingredients Tips:

Mirin (rice-based cooking wine) and nori (dried seaweed sheets) can be found in the Asian section of many grocery stores. Miso is refrigerated. If you cannot find miso paste, substitute 2 cups chicken stock + 2 cups clam juice.
You can substitute dried shiitake mushrooms for fresh in this recipe. Soak dried mushrooms in hot water for 30 minutes and strain before using.
You can use fresh or frozen shrimp. If using frozen shrimp, thaw before using.

Directions:

1. In a large saucepan, bring the water, soy sauce, miso paste, and mirin to a boil.

2. Reduce heat to a simmer and add scallions, mushrooms, and seaweed. Simmer for 3-4 minutes.

3. Add Āsh, one piece at a time.

4. Add shrimp, careful not to splash. Simmer until shrimp turns pink, 30 seconds to a minute.

Salt Woman:
A Story from the K´úutìim´é (Cochiti) People

The Cochiti people live in New Mexico. They are some of the descendants of the Ancestral Puebloans. This is the story of how they began adding salt to their food to make it taste better. The lake in the story might be Zuni Salt Lake. Zuni Salt Lake is sacred to Ma'l Okyattsik'i, the Zuni Salt Mother. Many of the Pueblo peoples in the area make pilgrimages to Zuni Salt Lake.

Once, long ago, Salt Woman came to Cochiti with her grandson, Salt Man. The two of them were very poor. They went house to house asking for food. But at each house, the People turned them away.

"We are too busy to give you food." After every house had refused them, Salt Woman found the place where all the children played. They were tossing bundles of corn husks and feathers back and forth, trying to keep them in the air. Salt Woman's neck, she wore a magic crystal. Salt Woman started swinging her necklace back and forth, back and forth, back and forth. As she swung the pendant, the children left their game and came to watch. Once she had their attention, she led them to a pinon tree.

"Here children," she said. "Let's play a game! Grab a branch and swing yourselves back and forth, back and forth, back and forth." Each child grasped a branch of the tree. As they did so, Salt Woman used her magic crystal to turn them all into chaparral jays. They were pretty little birds with blue feathers and lived in the pinon trees from then on. "This is because no one would give us anything to eat," Salt Woman told the birds.

"Ah ah ah ah," the birds cawed back at her. But Salt Woman and Salt Man had left.

Then Salt Woman and Salt Man came to Kewa. Once again, they asked for food. The People of Kewa welcomed Salt Woman and Salt Man. They shared generously and Salt Woman and Salt Man were grateful.

"You have been such wonderful hosts," Salt Woman said. "Thank you. I would like to give you a gift in return." She gave them a bit of her flesh and told them to add it to their food. They had never before tasted salt. They found that they loved the salty taste. It made their food taste better.

"I must go now. I shall go now to the southeast. If you wish to have more of my flesh, you will find me at a place three days' journey from here. If you must come, come quietly. There must be no laughing or singing. Make yourselves clean before you come."

And so, whenever the People needed salt, they traveled to the lake. They went quietly and made sure they were clean. And so they had flavor in all of their food.

Puebloan Hearty Soup

The Ancestral Puebloans lived in a desert environment and relied heavily on drought-resistant corn. One variety that thrived in the region was a type of blue corn, but you can use regular frozen corn for this recipe as well. For the meat, this tastes delicious with beef but venison, lamb, or goat would be more historically accurate.

GF, DF

4 servings

Level of Difficulty: 3

1 ½ hours

Ingredients:

1 tablespoon cooking oil

1 pound of meat, chopped into bite size pieces

1 bunch scallions, chopped

6 cups beef broth

1 teaspoon smoked paprika

½ teaspoon salt

12 ounces frozen corn

1 bunch fresh cilantro, chopped

Ingredients Tip:
You can buy pre-cut stew beef to make this step easier.

Directions:

1. Heat the oil in a large pot until shimmering. Add the meat and cook until browned, stirring frequently.

2. Add the chopped scallions and cook for about 2 minutes.

3. Pour in the broth, paprika, and salt.

4. Bring to a boil and then reduce heat to simmer and cover for about an hour until the meat is tender.

5. Add the corn and bring back to a boil. Simmer until the corn is cooked through.

6. Serve topped with chopped cilantro.

Turkey and Chochoyotes: Turkey and Dumplings

This recipe uses ingredients present in ancient Mesoamerica and includes a regional speciality from Oaxaca, Mexico. Some people call Oaxaca the cradle of Mexican cuisine. Indigenous cooking traditions are strong there. Chochoyotes, or corn dumplings, are a pre-Hispanic speciality in Oaxaca. They pair well with the turkey consumed by Mesoamericans for millennia.

GF, DF

8 servings

Level of Difficulty: 3

1 hour

Ingredients:

Soup:
1 small ancho chili, stemmed and seeded
1 ½ pounds turkey breast OR
1 ½ pounds boneless skinless chicken thighs
8 cups chicken broth
1 tablespoon salt
2 teaspoons smoked paprika
2 teaspoons oregano
1 teaspoon onion powder
½ teaspoon allspice
2 cans hominy, drained and rinsed
1 can black beans, drained and rinsed

Chochoyotes:
2 cups (240g) masa harina
2 cups warm water, more or less as needed

Cooking tip:
If you are worried the ancho chili will make this dish too spicy, add ¼ cup of puree at a time, tasting in between, until you reach the desired heat level.

Directions:

1. Soak the ancho chili in water during the next steps.
2. Heat cooking oil on medium heat in a large pot.
3. Brown the turkey on all sides, about 4 minutes per side.
4. Add the broth, salt, and spices and bring to a boil on medium high heat.
5. Reduce to a simmer, then cover and cook for 20-30 minutes until the turkey is tender.
6. Remove the turkey and let cool slightly on a cutting board.
7. In a blender, combine the soaked chili with ½ cup of liquid from the pot. Puree until smooth and pour into the pot.
8. Shred the turkey and return it to the pot. Add the hominy and black beans. Bring to a simmer.

To Make Chochoyotes

1. Mix the masa with 1 cup of water, stirring thoroughly. Then add more water, a few tablespoons at a time, until the mixture resembles wet clay.
2. Roll the masa into balls about 2 inches across, then press your thumb into the balls to make a depression. They will look almost like little balls. Add them to the soup as you make them. They should sink.
3. Ladle soup over the chochoyotes so that they are covered.
4. Cover and simmer for about 20 minutes. The chochoyotes are done when they have all Āoated to the top.

MESOAMERICA

Black Bean Tamales

The tamale dates back to around 7000 BC/BCE, when it was first made with wild maize. They were an important ritual food for the peoples of Mesoamerica from the Olmec to the Aztecs. Today, they are often part of Christian religious celebrations in Mexico. Why black beans? They were a staple of the Olmec diet, alongside maize.

GF; DF; V; V+

3 cups

Level of Difficulty: 2

50 minutes

Ingredients Tip:
You can order dry corn husks online or buy them at Hispanic grocery stores. They are sold by the pound, but you will only use about a quarter of them. You can also use the alternate method below.

Special Equipment:
Steamer (see alternate method)

Ingredients:

2 dozen corn husks

Filling:
1 can black beans, rinsed and drained

½ cup cilantro, minced

1 ancho chili, stem removed and chopped fine

1 tomatillo, diced

6 cloves garlic, peeled and minced (about 2 tablespoons)

1 tablespoon salt

½ teaspoon chili powder

Dough:
4 cups masa harina

1 teaspoon salt

4 cups warm water

½ cup vegetable shortening

Directions:

1. Bring a large pot of water to a boil. Turn it off and add the corn husks.

2. In a medium-sized pot, add all the filling ingredients and cover with water by about 2 inches.

3. Bring to a boil then reduce to a simmer. Simmer for about 30 minutes, until most of the liquid is gone.

4. Mix the masa harina and salt together in a large bowl. Add the warm water, one cup at a time, stirring in between each cup. Mix in the vegetable shortening. The dough should be easy to spread with a knife.

5. Put a steamer basket in the bottom of a large pot and fill with water just to the bottom of the steamer.

6. To fill the tamales, lay one husk in front of you, narrow side at the top. Spread a thin layer of masa dough over the bottom half of the husk, all the way to the edges.

7. Put about two tablespoons of the bean filling in the middle of the dough. Fold in the right side and then the left side. Then fold it over the top and leave the filled edge open. You can use strips of corn husk or string to tie them closed if you wish.

8. Place in the steamer, open side up and repeat until your filling and dough are gone. If you end up with extra dough, you can steam it as it is or use cheese as a filling.

9. Cover the tamales with extra husks to keep off the condensation from the steamer.

10. Cover and bring to a boil, then reduce to a simmer for about an hour. Listen for the sound of the water boiling and if it stops, add more water by carefully pouring it down the sides of the pot.

11. To check for doneness, carefully remove and unwrap a tamale. The tamale should pull away from the husk easily and without any sticking. If they are sticky, keep cooking.

12. Let sit for about ten minutes before serving. Serve plain, or with sour cream and salsa.

Alternate Cooking Method:

1. Preheat oven to 250 degrees.

2. Optional: use aluminum foil instead of corn husks.

3. Roll a piece of aluminum foil into a long tube. Then curve it into a 6 to 9 inch diameter ring. Set the ring in a dutch oven or oven-safe stock pot.

4. Pour water into the pot just to the top of the ring.

5. Arrange your foil packets vertically, using the ring to keep them upright and out of the water.

6. Put on the lid. Bake at 250 degrees for 1 to 1 ½ hours.

Food in Ancient
Scythia

The Scythians, who lived in Central Eurasia, were horse people. They wore some of the world's earliest pants because they were better for riding. They buried horses in their burial mounds. They dressed their horses in gorgeous clothes bedecked with gold. And they ate their horses. They drank horse blood, ate horse-meat, and made dairy products from mare's milk. They lived on mare's cheese and licorice root during long days in the saddle. But they were more than nomadic horse people.

Some Scythian groups grew grain, including wheat, millet, barley, and rye. They traded for tuna, sturgeon, onions, garlic, and beans. They also raised cattle and made a cheese that was something like quark. The Romans called it concretum.

Scythian stories were also passed down to later Eurasian cultures. The Nart Sagas tell the stories of great heroes and gods. Some of these tales describe meals. We have to be careful about using these as evidence, because they were oral folktales. They took on more modern flavors before folklorists wrote them down. One describes rifles, for example. You don't expect to find guns in ancient stories! But we can get a basic clue about food traditions from these stories. One story begins, "This happened in very olden times." It describes the skill of the Narts at making white wine. The Epics also describe dried kasha (buckwheat) and barley; honey; hot porridge with melted butter; cheese bread; golden apples; mutton; pears; goat meat; and cheese curds. They might have made porridge with any of the above grains.

How do we know what they ate? The Scythians left no written language. Much of our knowledge of them comes from Greek and Roman writing. The Greeks divided the Scythians into several categories. They claim the most barbaric Scythians ate human flesh. There is no actual evidence to back this up. The groups that roamed the land on horseback were only slightly less barbaric to the Greeks. But the Scythians who settled in one place to raise grain and bake bread? Those were more civilized people. The Greeks decided they were "Greco-Scythians."

Ancient Scythian Menu:

Breakfast:
Millet Porridge: *p.21*

Snacks:
Dried Apples: *p.42*
Quark: *p.57*

Dinner:
Ossetian Pies: *p.129*

Dessert:
Cherry Ossetian Pie: *p.182*

Drinks:
Grape Juice: *p.196*
Koumiss: *p.202*
Kefir: *p.205*

Fruits and Nuts:
Apples

Australia

Baked Catfish

Catfish is one of the most widely spread types of fish on the planet. They are found on every continent except for Antarctica. There aren't very many foods that Australia and the Americas have in common, but this is one! Aboriginal Australians have used fire for roasting fish over the millennia, but it's tasty baked in the oven too.

Ingredients:

4 catfish filets, about 6 ounces each

1 teaspoon salt

¼ teaspoon ground black pepper

Ingredients Tip:
In Australia, they use Tasmanian Pepperberry, also called Native Pepperberry. But ground black pepper works just fine!

Directions:

1. Preheat the oven to 400 degrees.

2. Pat the filets dry with a paper towel and sprinkle with salt and pepper.

3. Bake for about 20 minutes, until the flesh just flakes with a fork.

Note: If your filets are less than ¾ of an inch thick, they will cook in 10-15 minutes.

GF; DF

4 servings

Level of
Difficulty: 2

25 minutes

Ossetian Pies

Ossetian pies have ancient roots. They are mentioned in the Nart Sagas, which have their roots in Scythian mythology. Today Ossetian pies are still made in the Ossetia region of the country of Georgia. They are similar to a stuffed pizza and you can use prepared pizza dough as a shortcut. Just make sure to roll it very thin! This dough recipe makes two pies.

GF variation, V

2 pies

Level of
Difficulty: 3

3 hours

Ingredients:

Dough:

3 cups (450g) all-purpose flour plus more for dusting

2 ¼ teaspoons instant yeast (1 packet)

2 teaspoons salt

2 teaspoons sugar

1 cup warm water (about 110 degrees)

½ cup sour cream

1 egg

2 tablespoons olive oil

4 tablespoons butter

Fillings:

See p.131

Directions:

1. Mix together the flour, yeast, salt, sugar, water, sour cream, and egg. This works best with a mixer and paddle attachment, but can be done by hand. Mix together until everything is thoroughly combined and the dough is pulling away from the sides of the bowl. Then mix in the oil.

2. If the mixture is sticky, add additional flour a tablespoon at a time, mixing in between.

3. Turn the mixture out onto a floured surface. Form a ball with your hands and then fold it in half and press down. Rotate the dough halfway and repeat. Continue until the dough feels stretchy.

4. Put the dough in a greased bowl. Cover with a clean towel and let it rise in a warm place (70 degrees or warmer) for about 2 hours. It is done when it springs back after being pressed with a finger. Prepare fillings while the dough is rising.

5. Preheat oven to 450 degrees. Grease a baking sheet.

6. On a floured surface, divide the dough in half. Flatten the dough into a disc about 18" across.

7. Scoop the filling into the center of the dough.

8. Bring in one edge of the dough, folding it over the filling, and repeat, going around the edge.

9. When the filling is completely covered, carefully press down and flatten the filled dough until it is about a ½ inch thick.

10. Carefully transfer to a baking sheet.

11. Repeat for the second half of the dough.

12. Bake in the oven for 20-30 minutes, until golden brown. While the pies are baking, melt the butter.

13. Remove the pies from the oven and brush all over with melted butter. Let rest for five minutes and serve hot.

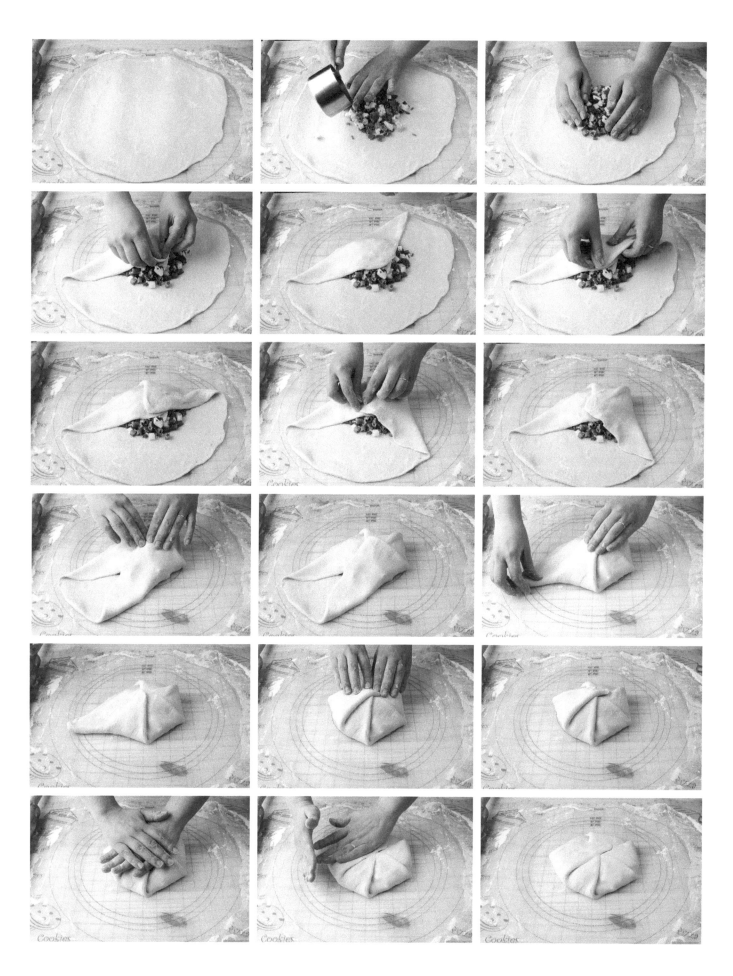

Fillings: Pick 2

Davondjin Filling:

Ingredients:

1 small bunch chives, finely chopped

1 bunch scallions, finely chopped

4 ounces feta cheese

Directions:

Mix together all the ingredients.

Kabushkadjin - Syht Filling:

Ingredients:

1 teaspoon olive oil

½ of a medium onion, diced

½ pound cabbage, finely chopped

¼ teaspoon salt

⅛ teaspoon ground black pepper

4 ounces feta cheese

Directions:

1. Heat the olive oil in a skillet on medium heat until shimmering.

2. Add the onions and cook, stirring, for about 5 minutes.

3. Add the cabbage, salt, and pepper and cook, stirring often, for 10 minutes.

4. Combine the vegetables and feta in a medium bowl.

Tsaharadjin Filling

Ingredients:

1 bunch beet greens

1 tablespoon olive oil

1 bunch chives, finely chopped

1 tablespoon chopped fresh cilantro or 1 teaspoon dried cilantro

6 ounces feta cheese

Directions:

1. Wash the beet greens and cut the leaves off the stems. Finely chop the leaves and stems separately.

2. Heat the oil in a skillet on medium heat until shimmering. Add the beet stems and saute for 5 minutes.

3. Add the beet leaves and stir until just wilted.

4. Remove from the heat and stir in the chives, cilantro, and cheese.

Gluten Free Variation

You can use gluten-free pizza dough and achieve a similar effect. Gluten-free flour cannot be substituted 1 to 1 in this recipe. Wholly Gluten Free Pizza Dough works very well.

Plakuntos: Ancient Greek Pizza

Plakuntos was an ancient Greek flatbread, made with oil, cheese, garlic, and herbs. It's very much like today's white pizzas!

GF Variation

2 twelve-inch pizzas

Level of Difficulty: 2

45 minutes (varies)

Ingredients:

Prepared pizza dough for 2 twelve-inch pizzas *(use a mix, buy prepared dough, or use your favorite crust recipe)*

1 cup shredded mozzarella cheese

2 cloves garlic, minced

1 teaspoon dried oregano

Directions:

1. Divide the dough and roll out the crusts.

2. Parbake crusts if instructed to do so.

3. Arrange the garlic evenly between both plakuntos.

4. Divide the cheese between both plakuntos, spreading it evenly across the circle.

5. Sprinkle 1 teaspoon of oregano across each plakuntos.

6. Bake according to crust instructions.

Food in Ancient
Australia

Baked Catfis

Warrigal Greens

Millet Flatbread

Aborigines used to eat thousands of species of plants and animals. Many are unique to Australia. These included large animals like kangaroos and emus. They also ate lizards, shellfish, fish, wild berries, wild fruits, and many kinds of seeds and bulbs. They ate platypus and wild bird eggs. Aborigines learned how to process and cook foods that were toxic if eaten fresh and raw. They baked their food in earth ovens or roasted it on coals. They ate all parts of animals, including muscle, fat, and organs. Aboriginal women gathered insects and plant foods. Many Aborigines ate honeypot ants as a source of sugar. These ants store a sweet nectar in their abdomen, expanding a special sac until it is the size of a small grape. Other insects served as valuable sources of protein. Entomophagy, or eating insects, is an age-old and global tradition.

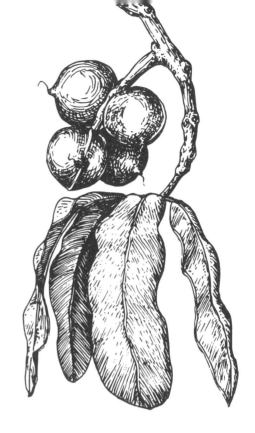

Australian Aborigines had little contact with other peoples for thousands of years. Their foods did not spread to other places. When white Europeans arrived to colonize Australia, they did not want to eat the local food. They attempted to erase Aboriginal culture, including the food.

Attitudes towards traditional foods are changing. The Aborigines of today eat about 40 different plant and animal species. They still hunt kangaroos and cook them using traditional methods. Today, people use the terms "bush food" or "bush tucker" to describe traditional foods. Bush tucker now shows up on the menu of fancy restaurants. Even kangaroo is common at Australian grocery stores. White Australians own most commercial bush food businesses. Some people are working towards more indigenous owned shops.

Due to the European bias against native Australian foods, most are not available in American grocery stores. Macadamia nuts are the most common Australian export today. The Australian recipes in this book are inspired by native Australian ingredients and traditional techniques, but are not direct reproductions of Australian Aboriginal dishes.

How do we know what they ate? Archaeology provides information. So do the living traditions of Australia's many Aboriginal cultures.

Ancient Australia Menu:

Breakfast:
Millet Flatbread: *p.61*
Millet Porridge: *p.21*

Snacks:
Macadamia Nuts

Dinner:
"Warrigal" Greens: *p.95*
Baked Catfish: *p.127*

Drink:
Honey Water: *p.193*

Fruits and Nuts:

With the exception of macadamia nuts and bananas (a variety native to northern Australia), indigenous Australian fruits and vegetables are difficult to find in the United States. European colonizers gave many of these plants common names based on their resemblance to fruits and vegetables they had back home. Australia has a dazzling array of edible native plants. This list is mostly informational, although you can order foods made from these plants online.

Fruits

Quandong
Kutjera
Muntries
Riberry
Davidson's plum
Finger lime
Boab
Cedar bay cherry
Kakadu lime
Cluster fi
Wongi
Blue tongue
Tanjong
Great morinda
Native gooseberry
Kakadu plum
Johnstone's River satinash
Fibrous saunash
Lady apple
Native caper/caperbush
Wild orange
Wild passionfruit
Bush plum, conkerberry
Desert lime
Ruby saltbush
Desert fi
Doubah, bush banana
Emer apple
Bitter quandong
Akudjura, Australian desert raisin
Bush tomato
Solanum centrale
Solanum cleistogarnum
Solanum ellipticum
Lemon aspen

White aspen
Herbert river cherry
Rose myrtle
Midyim
Pigface
Dooja (citrus)
Small-leafed tamarind
Botwarra
Sandpaper fi
Zig zag vine
Hala fruit
Burdekin plum
Illawarra plum
Black apple
Broad-leaf bramble
Brush cherry
Magenta lilly pilly
Yellow plum
Native cranberry
Pine heat berry
Mountain blueberry
Apple dumplings (berry)
Mountain currant
Native currant--raw or stewed
Shortstem flaxilily berrie
Spreading flaxlily berrie
Blue flax lily berrie
Climbing saltbush
Kangaroo apple
Native pepper
Sweet apple-berry
Purple apple-berry
Common apple-berry
Karkalla
Native cherry
Snow berry
Muntries
Pink-flowered native raspberr
White elderberry

Vegetables

Purple yam
Round yam
Pencil yam, long yam
Spike rush
Water spinach
Lotus
Water lily
Parakeelya
Bush potato
Peppercresses
Large pig weed
Sea celery
Scurvy weed
Scrambling lily
Warrigal greens (like spinach)
Wild parsnip
Scrub nettle
Flinders island celery
Grey saltbush
Milkmaids--roasted tuber
Wombat berry
Murnong
Neptunes necklace (seaweed)

Nuts

Cycald palm seeds (detoxified and used in bush bread)
Australian cashew
Sea almond
Bunya nut
Atherton almond
Bush nut
Peanut tree

Roman Fowl with Green Sauce

This recipe is by the Roman cookbook author, Apicius. This recipe, and many others, call for a sauce called garum. The Romans put this sauce on everything! It was a fermented fish sauce. For our recipes, we are just using fish sauce. We have substituted grape juice for the wine in the original recipe. Here is the recipe in Latin:

Ius viride in avibus: Piper, careum, spicam indicam, cuminum, folium, condimenta viridia omne genus, dactilum, mel, acetum, vinum modice, liquamen et oleum.

GF, DF

1 cup sauce; 4 chicken breasts

Level of Difficulty: 3

20-40 minutes

Ingredients:

4 boneless skinless chicken breasts or thighs

1 teaspoon salt

1 tablespoon olive oil

1 bunch parsley, minced

6 pitted dates

2 tablespoons white wine vinegar

2 tablespoons olive oil

1 tablespoon honey

1 tablespoon grape juice

1 teaspoon Herbes de Provence

1 teaspoon Āsh sauce

⅛ teaspoon caraway seeds (*careum*)

⅛ teaspoon ground cumin (*cuminum*)

⅛ teaspoon dried oregano

⅛ teaspoon ground black pepper (*Piper*)

⅛ teaspoon dried thyme

Special Equipment:
Blender
Mallet or Meat Tenderizer

Directions:

1. Pat the chicken dry with a paper towel.

2. Put the chicken on a cutting board and cover with a sheet of plastic wrap. Pound with a mallet until it is an even thickness all over.

3. Discard plastic wrap and sprinkle salt all over both sides of the chicken.

4. Heat olive oil in a skillet on medium heat until shimmering.

5. Carefully add the chicken breasts to the pan, cooking in two batches if necessary. Cook until golden brown underneath and flip over, about ten minutes. Cook until the bottom is golden, about another ten minutes.

6. Inset Tip: If you aren't sure if chicken is cooked, pierce it with a knife. The juices will run clear when the chicken is cooked. If you have a cooking thermometer, the center should be 165 degrees.

7. Meanwhile, put all of the remaining ingredients in a blender or food processor and puree until smooth.

8. Serve the chicken topped with the green sauce.

Note: This green sauce also tastes delicious with the honeyed pork on p.155

Chicken Yassa

The Ghana Empire, or Wagadou, was located partially in modern day Senegal. Chicken yassa is a more recent traditional dish in Senegal that has become popular throughout West Africa. It's not a complicated dish to cook, but it does require plenty of time for the onions to caramelize for the best flavor. It seems like a lot of onions, but they will cook down. Traditionally the dish is quite spicy, but we have reduced the amount of chili powder and eliminated any hot peppers. Chili powder is part of the recipe, but would have been unknown in ancient Africa. All the heat would have come from black pepper. Feel free to add some spice back in if you like! In Senegal today, fish yassa is also popular. You can substitute grilled fish for the browned chicken.

GF, DF

6 servings

Level of
Difficulty: 3

3-4 hours

Ingredients:

2 pounds boneless skinless chicken thighs

7 onions, cut in half and sliced thinly

½ cup lemon juice

¼ cup Dijon mustard

1 head of garlic, peeled and minced *(10-12 cloves, about 6 tablespoons minced)*

¼ teaspoon ground black pepper

6 tablespoons olive oil

1 preserved lemon, chopped *(recipe on p.219)*

2 cups chicken stock

2 teaspoons chili powder

Ingredients Tip:
Preserved lemons are available at gourmet markets and international grocery stores.

Directions:

1. In a large bowl, mix together the lemon juice, mustard, 3 tablespoons garlic, and ½ teaspoon black pepper.

2. Add the chicken and onions to the bowl and stir, making sure everything is coated in the marinade. Cover and marinate for at least 2 hours or overnight.

3. Remove the chicken from the marinade and chop into bite sized pieces.

4. Heat 3 tablespoons olive oil in a stock pot over medium heat until shimmering. Add the chicken in batches, making sure not to overcrowd the bottom of the pot. Brown chicken on all sides and remove to a bowl.

5. Heat the remaining three tablespoons of olive oil in the pan and add the onions and remaining marinade. Reduce the heat to medium low and cook the onions for 30-40 minutes, stirring frequently to avoid burning. The onions should turn golden brown and shrink down.

6. Add the remaining garlic and cook for about 30 seconds.

7. Return chicken and accumulated juices to pot along with the chicken stock, chili powder and preserved lemon.

8. Bring to a boil then reduce and simmer uncovered for 30 minutes or until the sauce is almost fully absorbed. Serve over rice.

Food in Ancient East Africa

Chicken Suqaar

Sabayaad

The Kingdoms of Punt and Kush existed so long ago that most of their food traditions have vanished. With historians unsure of the exact location of Punt, even archaeology is a limited tool. Luckily, they both had connections to Ancient Egypt.

We know that ancient Egypt shared some food practices with these kingdoms. When Egyptians invaded Kush, their culture began to replace many traditional cultural elements. That likely meant the food became Egyptianized too. So what did they eat exactly? We don't know. We could cook ancient Egyptian dishes. We can also look at modern Ethiopian recipes. Ethiopia's culinary history is unique among African countries. It lacks a history of European colonization. Some people say Ethiopian cooking is the purest of African cooking. If you take away the ingredients that come from the Western Hemisphere, you might end up with something closer to the diet of the ancient people of Kush.

How about Punt? The Egyptians wrote about non-edible goods they imported from Punt. They did not write much about the food. They wrote: Punt had "everything found in Egypt" to eat. That list included beer, bread, wine, meat, and fruit. If we use those ingredients with traditional Somali cooking, we can try to recreate the meals of Punt.

How do we know what they ate? We look at the interactions of East African nations with cultures who wrote about them. We have archaeology in the case of Kush. Archaeological evidence tells us about agriculture. We know the foods native to the region and how long people have cultivated them. We can also look to the cooking traditions of the region today to trace the ancient roots of today's dinners.

Kush Menu:

Breakfast:
Millet Porridge: *p.21*

Snacks:
Millet Flatbread: *p.61*
Ayib: *p.59*

Dinner:
Collard Greens: *p.94*
Doro Wat: *p.153*

Drink:
Honey Water: *p.193*

Punt Menu:

Breakfast:
Chickpea Pancakes: *p.34*

Snacks:
Sabaayad: *p.60*

Dinner:
Turmeric Rice: *p.93*
Chicken Suqaar: *p.143*

Dessert:
Kashata: *p.165*

Drink:
Biyo Cambe: *p.195*

Fruits and Nuts:
Because of the trade and interactions between Egypt and the Kingdoms of Punt and Kush, you could use fruits and vegetables from Egypt's menu. The records of Egypt's visit to Punt describe the kingdom as having similar fruits and vegetables.

Bananas
Coconut (late introduction)
Dates
Mango (late 9th century AD/CE)
Sweet Cassava

PUNT (SOMALIA)

Chicken Suqaar

Suqaar is the Somali word for "sauteed meat" and can be used for chicken, beef, goat, or lamb. This dish pairs well with bariis xawaash leb *(turmeric rice, pg.93)* and sabaayad *(pg.60)*. Today, this dish often contains spicy peppers and squash, but these ingredients were still only to be found in the Western Hemisphere during ancient times.

GF; DF

4 servings

Level of
Difficulty: 3

30 minutes

Ingredients:

2 teaspoons olive oil or ghee *(if not dairy free)*

1 small onion, diced

1 teaspoon ground cumin

1 teaspoon salt

½ teaspoon ground black pepper

1 to 1 ½ pound boneless skinless chicken thighs, cut into bite-sized pieces

2 teaspoons lemon juice

1 teaspoon white vinegar

1 teaspoon chopped fresh cilantro

Directions:

1. Heat the oil or ghee on medium heat and add the onions. Stir frequently and cook until translucent, about 5 minutes.

2. Add the seasonings and cook for about 30 seconds, stirring constantly.

3. Stir in the chicken and saute until the meat is cooked through, about 15 minutes.

4. Turn oﬀ the heat and stir in the lemon juice, vinegar, and cilantro.

5. Serve with rice or ﬂatbread.

Food in Ancient
Mesoamerica

Tortillas

Turkey
Thlacos

Ahuaca-Mulli

Most of our information about pre-colonial Mesoamerican cooking comes from archaeology. Historians use the oldest dated artifacts to determine when people started to eat different foods. Many of the foods grown in ancient Mesoamerica are still popular today. Do you like maize (corn) or chocolate? Then thank a Mesoamerican!

The Three Sisters Garden is one of the greatest agricultural achievements of the indigenous peoples of the Americas. The relationship between maize, beans, and squash is beneficial both in the field and on the table. The technique dates back thousands of years. Humans first domesticated corn in Mesoamerica around seven thousand years ago. Then followed by squash and beans. When planted together, they make the Three Sisters. Paleobotanists believe people planted the first Three Sisters gardens in Mexico around 3,500 years ago. The practice spread into the American southwest and across North America. Many Native American nations have legends about the origins of the Three Sisters. The practice was widespread across North America.

What makes this trio of vegetables such a perfect combination? Gardeners call this method companion planting. Sometimes, two or more types of plants grow better when planted together. At the beginning of the planting season, they plant corn in hills (mounded up piles of dirt). Later, they plant beans and squash in the same hills. Why hills? Hills provide better drainage. The better exposure to the warmth of the sun fosters faster growth. The corn supports the runners of the beans. In turn, the beans fix nitrogen in the soil. Nitrogen is an important nutrient for many plants. Without it, the plants turn yellow and fail to thrive. Both the corn and squash thrive in the richer soil. They are nutrient-greedy plants, and they use a lot of nitrogen to grow. The broad leaves of the squash prevent the soil from drying out too quickly, and prevent weeds from growing. The three sisters work together for human health too! Humans need nine essential amino acids to be healthy. A complete protein includes all nine amino acids. After the harvest, the corn and beans form a complete protein when served together at the table.

How about chocolate? The scientific name for the cacao tree is theobroma cacao, which means food of the gods. Do you feel like chocolate is the food of the gods? Some Mesoamerican legends tell stories of how the gods gave cacao seeds to humans (see p.212).

The Olmecs were the first to grow cacao trees and turn their seeds into a drink. We don't know exactly how it started. Here's one theory. Someone was eating the fruit of the cacao tree, which has a similar flavor to other tropical fruits. They were spitting out the seeds, maybe into a fire. The roasted seeds smelled delicious. Maybe these seeds were edible! Even so, it's a long process to make the seeds into chocolate. You have to wonder how someone figured it out. We don't know much about chocolate culture in the Olmec civilization. We know they drank it out of special round jars used only for drinking chocolate. Later, Aztec and Mayan nobility enjoyed drinking chocolate too.

The Mesoamericans both hunted and raised animals for food. They raised rabbits, turkeys, and dogs, and hunted deer and wild birds. Alongside the Three Sisters, they raised tomatoes, chili peppers, amaranth, and avocados. These ingredients are still popular in Central American cooking today!

How do we know what they ate? The Spanish wrote a lot about food from their earliest arrival. Their writing provides a snapshot at the moment of contact. Oral tradition preserved other pieces of food history, like stories about the Three Sisters. The Olmecs and Mayans left behind written language, although no one has been able to translate Olmec yet.

Mesoamerican Menu:

Breakfast:

Atole: *p.214*

Snacks:

Popcorn: *p.43*

Dinner:

Maize and Squash Salad: *p.77*

Black Bean Tamales: *p.125*

Turkey and Chochoyotes: *p.123*

Thlacos: *p.149*

Dessert:

Champurrado: *p.185*

Drinks:

Hot Chocolate: *p.213*

Fruits and Nuts:

Avocados

Papaya

Babylonian Lamb Stew

The licorice and juniper for this dish can be tricky to source, but it's well worth the effort. The recipe is based on a Babylonian tablet held by Yale University and given the number YBC 4644. The tablet has a number of recipes carved into it, including the following original text translated from Akkadian by Jean Bottero and Teresa Lavender Fagan.

"Leg of mutton, but no other meat is used. Prepare water; add fat; dodder [wild licorice] as desired; salt to taste, cypress [juniper berries]; onion, samidu [semolina]; cumin; coriander; leek and garlic, mashed with kisimmu [sour cream or yogurt]. It is ready to serve."

GF Variation

servings

Level of Difficulty: 3

2.5 hours

Ingredients:

1 tablespoon olive oil

1 ½ to 1 ¾ pound lamb on the bone

1 leek, halved, rinsed thoroughly, and sliced thinly.

2 teaspoons ground licorice root or 1 teaspoon anise extract

1 yellow onion, halved and thinly sliced

2 teaspoons minced garlic

1 teaspoon salt

6 juniper berries (optional)

1 teaspoon cumin

1 teaspoon ground coriander

4 cups beef broth

4 tablespoons flour

1 cup yogurt

Ingredients Tip:

If you don't eat lamb, you can substitute the same amount of beef.

Directions:

1. Heat olive oil on medium heat until shimmer, then sear the meat on all sides until browned. Set meat aside.

2. Add leeks and onions to the hot pan and cook until translucent, about 5 minutes.

3. Add garlic and spices and cook for another 30 seconds.

4. Return the lamb to the pan, nestling it into the onion mixture. Add beef broth to cover the meat.

5. Bring the mixture to a boil then reduce to a simmer and cover.

6. Simmer for about 2 hours until the meat falls off the bone.

7. Remove the meat to a cutting board and cut or shred the meat.

8. Measure the flour into a small bowl, then slowly add one cup of hot broth from the stew, whisking constantly, until smooth (this is called a slurry).

9. Add your slurry back to the stew and stir until thickened.

10. Turn off the heat. Remove about ¼ cup of broth from the pot and slowly whisk it into the yogurt in a small bowl. This is called tempering and keeps the yogurt from curdling. Stir the tempered yogurt back into the stew.

Gluten Free Variation:

In Step 8, whisk together 3 tablespoons cornstarch with 2 tablespoons cold water before adding it to the stock. Repeat as necessary to reach a stew-like consistency.

Thlacos: Turkey

Thlacos, known by us as tacos, date back to the Aztec period or possibly earlier. Turkey was one possible Ālling. Beans are another. Chopped turkey would be most authentic, but ground turkey is widely available. Mesoamerican peoples have used the seasonings in this recipe for thousands of years. Top with ahuaca-mulli *(pg. 222)* and serve on corn tortillas *(pg. 67)*. As an interesting note: the Mesoamericans did not use any cooking oils prior to Spanish arrival. They would have Āre-roasted the meat.

Ingredients:

GF; DF

8

1 pound turkey, ground or sliced into thin strips.

1 teaspoon allspice

½ teaspoon paprika

¼ teaspoon salt

Vegetable oil

Directions:

1. Combine the meat and seasonings in a bowl, making sure they are completely mixed.

2. Heat about a tablespoon of vegetable oil in a skillet on medium heat.

3. When the oil is shimmering, add the meat. Cook until brown, stirring frequently.

4. Serve warm.

Level of
Difficulty: 3

20 minutes

MESOAMERICA

Thlacos: Black Bean

For a vegetarian taco, use this black bean filling. It tastes delicious topped with ahuaca-mulli (p.222) and maize and squash salad (p.77)

GF; DF; V; V+

8

Level of
Difficulty: 3

30 minutes

Ingredients:

2 cans black beans, drained and rinsed

1/2 cup vegetable broth

1 tablespoon tomato paste

1 teaspoon allspice

1 teaspoon paprika

1 teaspoon onion powder

1/2 teaspoon salt

Directions:

1. Combine everything in a medium saucepan and bring to a boil.

2. Reduce to a simmer and cook, uncovered, for about 20 minutes.

3. Stir frequently until the liquid is almost completely gone.

4. Serve on corn tortillas.

KUSH (ETHIOPIA)

Ancient Doro Wat

Doro Wat is a dish for special occasions in Ethiopia today. The hostess breaks oﬀ a piece of injera, wraps it around a bite of the chicken, and places it in the mouth of each guest as a way to welcome them. This is called gursha. Authentic Doro Wat is a much more complex dish with far more ingredients. This version is simpler and uses ingredients available during ancient times. It can be served with injera or other ﬂat breads.

GF

4 servings

Level of
Difficulty: 3

1 ½ hours

Ingredients:

1 fryer chicken, cut into parts with skin removed

1 cup water

1 teaspoon lemon juice

1 teaspoon salt

6 eggs

1 onion, chopped

¼ cup butter

1 cup chicken broth

1 teaspoon ginger

1 teaspoon paprika

½ teaspoon garlic powder

1 teaspoon ground black pepper

Ingredients Tip:
You can often purchase a package of a whole chicken cut into parts or bone-in chicken quarters. This is the easiest thing to do! Look for about a 2 pound package.

Directions:

1. Make several shallow cuts into each piece of chicken.

2. Put chicken in a bowl with the lemon juice, salt, and water. Refrigerate for 30 minutes.

3. Meanwhile, hard boil the eggs. Bring a pot of water to a boil on high and add the eggs carefully with a slotted spoon. Cover and simmer for ten minutes. Fill a bowl with ice water. Use the slotted spoon to transfer the eggs to the ice water.

4. Put the butter in a soup pot and heat on medium heat until the butter is melted and starting to brown.

5. Add the onion and cook until brown around the edges, about ten minutes. Stir frequently.

6. Add the spices and stir for about 30 seconds.

7. Dry the chicken parts and add them to the pot.

8. Add the broth.

9. Bring to a boil then reduce the heat to a simmer. Cover and cook for 20 minutes.

10. Peel the eggs. Add them to the pot, making sure they are covered in sauce. Cook for another 20 minutes.

11. Remove the chicken and take the meat oﬀ the bones. Shred meat with a fork and return to the pot.

12. Simmer uncovered for another 20 minutes until the sauce has thickened. Serve.

Babylonian Hen with Herbs

The people of ancient Mesopotamia loved boiling their meat, and it was their foundational cooking technique. A set of Babylonian tablets included a couple dozen "recipes." Written for the experienced cook, they had few guidelines for techniques and were little more than a list of ingredients. Here is the original recipe, translated from the original Akkadian by John Lawton. Tarru-bird is any kind of fowl. The mutton is used to make a broth for boiling the meat.

"Tarru-Bird Stew: Meat from a fresh leg of mutton is needed. Boil the water, throw fat in. Dress the tarru. Add coarse salt as needed. Hulled cake of malt. Squeeze onions, samîdu, leek, garlic and add to pot along with milk. After cutting up the tarru, plunge them in stock. Then place them back in the pot. To be brought out for carving."

GF variation

4 servings

Level of Difficulty: 3

45-60 minutes

Ingredients:

⅓ cup pomegranate juice

¼ cup red wine vinegar

2 tablespoons honey

⅓ cup olive oil plus additional for cooking

2 ¼ tsp ground coriander

1 teaspoon ground cumin

1 teaspoon ground cinnamon

1 teaspoon salt

⅛ teaspoon ground black pepper

2 pounds boneless skinless chicken thighs

4 cups chicken stock

3 tablespoons butter

1 shallot, minced

1 leek, cleaned and thinly sliced

12 cloves garlic, peeled and minced (about 1 head, 6 tablespoons)

½ cup Greek yogurt at room temperature

5 oz baby spinach

1-3 tablespoons Āour or cornstarch

Special Equipment:
Blender (optional)

Directions:

1. Whisk together the pomegranate juice, red wine vinegar, and honey. Slowly add the olive oil, whisking constantly.

2. Stir together the mint, coriander, cumin, cinnamon, salt, and pepper.

3. Pat the chicken dry and rub with the spice mix.

4. Melt 1 tablespoon of butter in a large stockpot.

5. Add the chicken and brown on all sides. Remove to a dish.

6. Add 1 tablespoon of butter to the pot and saute the shallot and leek for about 5 minutes.

7. Add the garlic and saute for 1 minute.

8. Return the chicken and any juices to the pot with the chicken stock and pomegranate dressing and stir. Bring to a boil over high heat.

9. Reduce to a simmer and cook covered for about 20 minutes.

10. ake about ¼ cup of broth from the pot and slowly add it to the yogurt in a small bowl, whisking constantly. This is called tempering and keeps the yogurt from curdling.

11. 1Gradually stir the tempered yogurt into the pot.

12. Add your spinach to the stock and simmer until it is just wilted. Use a slotted spoon to remove the spinach to a serving dish.

13. In a small bowl, whisk the Āour with about ¼ cup of broth and pour into the pot. If you are using cornstarch, whisk together 3 tablespoons cornstarch with 2 tablespoons cold water before adding it to the stock. Repeat as necessary to reach a gravy-like consistency. Using a blender, puree until smooth if desired.

14. Serve as follows: a layer of spinach, a piece of chicken, and gravy spooned over the top.

Roman Honey - Roasted Pork

"There is no animal who furnishes more variety to the tongue: its meat provides nearly fifty flavors, but that of the other animals only one." --Pliny the Elder

This simple recipe from Apicius is delicious! The Romans loved sweet, sour, and salty flavors so the simplicity of this recipe is unusual. Apicius recommended this for any meat, but we found it particularly tasty with pork tenderloin.

GF, DF

4 servings

Level of Difficulty: 3

30 minutes

Ingredients:

1 pork tenderloin, about 1.5 pounds

1-2 teaspoons salt

2 tablespoons honey

Directions:

1. Preheat oven to 425 degrees.

2. Pat the pork dry and salt generously.

3. Cook in a roasting pan for 25-30 minutes, until the temperature is about 145. Turn off the oven.

4. Brush with honey and return to the still-hot oven for five minutes.

5. Remove from oven and brush pan juices and dripped honey back over the pork.

6. Slice and serve.

Rou Jia Mo: Chinese Beef Sandwiches

Some say that this is the world's oldest sandwich. We can't confirm that but we can confirm that it is delicious! Modern versions are often spicy, including hot peppers native to the Americas. We've made this version more authentic by eliminating the hot peppers. The star anise can be tricky to find, but is well worth it for the flavor. To save time on this dish, we have substituted English muffins for the traditional buns.

GF Variation

6 sandwiches

Level of Difficulty: 4

2 hours

Ingredients:

2 teaspoons cooking oil, divided

2 pounds top round beef, cut into 1 inch cubes

2 pieces star anise or 1 ½ teaspoons anise seeds

2 bay leaves

1 teaspoon ground cinnamon

1 teaspoon ground cumin

¾ teaspoon ground coriander

½ teaspoon ground black pepper

½ teaspoon ground cardamom

½ teaspoon ground ginger

1 yellow onion, thinly sliced

3 cloves garlic, peeled and minced (about 1 tablespoon)

¼ cup rice vinegar

3 tablespoons soy sauce (GF if needed), divided

2 tablespoons honey

6 English muffins (GF if needed)

1 cup minced fresh cilantro, washed and stems removed

Directions:

1. In a Dutch oven or heavy-bottomed pan, heat half of the oil on medium-high heat until the oil shimmers.

2. Add the beef to the pan, leaving space in between the pieces. Work in batches if necessary.

3. Sear the meat, turning to make sure it browns on all sides.

4. Remove the meat from the pan, setting aside in a bowl.

5. Add the onions to the pan and cook until softened, about 5 minutes. Add garlic and cook 30 seconds more.

6. Return the beef and any juices to the pan along with the spices, vinegar, 2 tablespoons soy sauce, honey, and 2 cups of water.

7. Raise the heat and bring to a boil.

8. Cover the pan, reduce the heat, and simmer until the beef is tender enough to pull apart with a fork, about 1 ½ hours.

9. Strain the mixture, reserving the broth. Remove bay leaves and star anise pieces.

10. In a separate pot, bring the broth to a boil. Boil for about 5 minutes, until the mixture has reduced by about half.

11. In the original pan, heat the rest of the cooking oil then stir in the beef mixture and the remaining soy sauce. Stir to break up the beef. Cook for about 2 minutes.

12. Toast the English muffins in a toaster or toaster oven.

13. Toss the beef and broth together in a large bowl.

14. Divide the beef between the English muffins and top with cilantro.

DESSERTS

Sweeteners

Did you know that the average American today eats 22 teaspoons of added sugar each day? That's about 57 pounds per year! Our ancestors would have a hard time imagining such easy access to sweets.

The first sweetener was honey. The honeybees who provide most of our honey today are native to Eurasia. People collected honey from wild bees in Africa and the Americas. The Mayans domesticated their own native species of honey-producing bees. In Europe, honey collection dates back at least 10,000 years. In New Zealand, the Maori people used honey made from the nectar of the Manuka tree to treat wounds.

Various legends around the world sprung up around this natural sweetener. In Ancient Rome, the pious offered honey to the gods to prevent volcanic eruptions. Perhaps the people of Pompeii were stingy with their honey! The Greeks and the Romans believed the gods grew up on honey, as well as ambrosia and nectar. The Romans even had a goddess of honey: Mellona. The Mayans had a honey god too: Ah-Muzen-Cab. The Egyptians believed that honey came from the tears of the sun god, Ra. That gives new meaning to "Re, a drop of golden sun!" In Australia, the Moon herself was drawn down from the sky in search of honey. Honey itself is a god in the Vedas of India.

In New Guinea eight thousand years ago, people began cultivating a tall grass with thick stems. Its stems were soft and sweet to chew on. Polynesian traders carried this sugarcane east to Hawaii and west to India by 3000 BC/BCE. In India, cane sugar was processed into a rough form of granulated sugar starting around 400 BC/BCE. Indian trade took sugar to China. Alexander the Great brought "honey powder" back from his Indian campaign. According to the Greek physician Dioscorides, it was "a kind of concentrated honey, called saccharon, found in canes in India and Arabia, like in consistency to salt, and brittle to be broken between the teeth."

Maple syrup is a sweetener with a limited range and wide popularity. Sugar-producing maples grow only in Canada and the northeastern United States. Their sweet sap runs in the part of the year with cold nights and warm days. Native American nations in the area have several stories about how they came to make maple syrup. You can find legends about maple syrup on p.26.

Mazamorra Morada: Two Ways

The origins of Mazamorra Morada are unclear, but date back to before Spanish colonization of Peru. This dessert starts similar to the drink Chicha Morada. We have provided a shortcut here. First is the more traditional recipe, then the shortcut.

GF; DF; V; V+

8 servings

Level of Difficulty: 3-4

3 hours

Traditional Recipe:
Ingredients:

3 pounds of dried purple corn, on or oﬀ the ear

3 cloves

3 cinnamon sticks

1 pineapple, peeled and chopped into bite size pieces, peel and core reserved

1 granny smith apple, peeled, cored, and chopped into bite size pieces, core and peels reserved

9 cups water

½ cup prunes

½ cup dried apricots

1 ½ cups sugar

½ cup potato starch

Juice of 1 lime (about 2 tablespoons)

Directions:

1. Combine the corn, spices, peels, and cores in a pot with water. Bring to a boil over high heat then cover and reduce to a simmer. Simmer for about an hour, or until you have about six cups of liquid.

2. Carefully strain the mixture, reserving the liquid and discarding the solids.

3. Return the liquid to the pot along with the fresh and dried fruit and sugar. Bring to a boil then reduce to a simmer for 20 minutes.

4. Carefully remove about a cup of liquid from the pot. Whisk in the potato starch until dissolved and then add back to the pan.

5. Cook until thick, about 5 minutes.

6. Stir in the lime juice.

7. Serve warm or chilled.

Simple Recipe:
Ingredients:

16 ounces Chicha Morada (from a bottle, prepared from a powder, or made from scratch)

¼ cup cornstarch

6 dried apricots, chopped

Ground cinnamon

Directions:

1. Whisk the cornstarch into the chicha morada in a medium saucepan.

2. Cook on medium high until thick.

3. Stir in apricots.

4. Sprinkle with cinnamon and serve warm.

Ingredients Tip:

Purple corn and Chicha Morada can be found at Hispanic markets or online.

INDIA

Murmura Ladoo

In our house, these bars reminded the kids of a certain marshmallow and rice cereal bar. Murmura Ladoo is more properly shaped into balls, but the bar form is easier to make when dealing with hot sugar. Preserved ladoo made of barley, wheat, and chickpeas were found in the ruins at Harappa. This sweet version is a popular traditional treat in India today.

GF; V

9 bars

Level of Difficulty: 3

40 minutes

Ingredients:

3 cups murmura (puffed rice)

1 teaspoon butter or ghee *(see ghee recipe on p. 217)*

1 cup (150g) brown sugar or jaggery

¼ cup water

Special Equipment:
Cooking thermometer (optional)

Ingredients Tips:
You can substitute crisped rice cereal for the murmura. It will have slightly less crunch but still taste delicious. Jaggery can be found at international grocery stores as a powder or in balls.

Ingredients Notes:
In India, they use a type of brown sugar called jaggery. If you have access to a good international market, go for it! You can also order it online. Regular brown sugar works just as well. Because of the simple ingredients in this recipe, make sure you are using either homemade or high quality ghee.

Directions:

1. Preheat the oven to 200 degrees and toast the puffed rice in a 9x9 baking dish for 20 minutes, stirring halfway through. Pour the rice into a large bowl and set aside to cool.

2. Grease the baking dish.

3. In a 2 quart pan, combine the butter, brown sugar, and water. Bring to a boil on high heat.

4. Boil until the mixture reaches the soft ball stage (see inset).

5. Remove from heat and stir quickly into the puffed rice. Make sure the rice is fully coated.

6. Scrape the mixture into the baking dish. Use a spatula to press it down into the pan. Dip the spatula in water if the mixture is too sticky.

7. Let set for five minutes then cut into nine pieces and serve.

To test the sugar without a thermometer, use a spoon to drop a small amount of the mixture into a bowl of water and try to form it into a ball with your fingers. If it stays in slippery threads, it needs to cook longer. If you have a thermometer, cook until the mixture reaches 240 degrees.

Kashata: Coconut Candy

Kashata is a type of candy popular in East Africa within Swahili culture. The Swahili people are the descendants of the Bantu, a people who migrated from West to East Africa about 2000 years ago. The name "Swahili" comes from an Arabic word meaning "coast," describing their region. They call themselves "Waungwana" which means "civilized ones."

GF; DF; V; V+

12 pieces

Level of Difficulty: 3

1 ½ hours

Ingredients:

2 ½ cups desiccated coconut (unsweetened coconut Āakes)

1 cup sugar

½ teaspoon ground cardamom

½ teaspoon cinnamon

1 teaspoon vanilla

Special Equipment:

Cooking Thermometer

Directions:

1. Grease a 9x9 baking dish.

2. Soak the desiccated coconut in ½ cup water. Stir together and soak until the coconut absorbs the water.

3. Meanwhile, mix the sugar with ¾ cup water in a saucepan and bring to a boil.

4. Boil for four minutes. Cook until the temperature reaches 230 degrees or soft ball stage (see p.163)

5. Turn the heat to low. Strain the coconut, pressing out excess moisture with a spoon.

6. Add the coconut, cardamom, and cinnamon to the sugar syrup and cook on low, stirring frequently. Continue to cook until the coconut has absorbed most of the syrup and the mixture pulls away from the pan.

7. Remove from heat and stir in the vanilla.

8. Press the coconut mixture into the baking dish.

9. Let sit for at least an hour or overnight, until it is Ārm enough to slice.

Food in Ancient Egypt

Grape Juice

Lentil Salad

Egyptian Barley Bread

Falafel

Egyptian Dried Spiced Beef

Yogurt

Dried Apples

Ancient Egyptian history spans thousands of years. Over that time, diets changed a little bit. But some things were universal. Both adults and children drank beer throughout the time of the pharaohs. The lower class got much-needed nutrients from beer. Wages were often paid in beer and bread. Beer was an important part of offerings to the gods. But this is not the beer most adults are familiar with today. It was cloudy and had solid sprouted grain floating in it. It also had a lower alcohol content than most modern beers. It contained tetracycline. Tetracycline is an antibiotic that wouldn't be available for thousands of years. You might think of beer as an ancient Egyptian health food!

What else did the Egyptians eat besides beer and bread? Well, they ate some fruits and vegetables you might find familiar. They ate celery, lettuce, scallions (green onions), cucumbers, melons, grapes, figs, and dates. They also ate papyrus! For meat, wealthy Egyptians ate beef, while the less wealthy ate goat, sheep, and pork. Almost everyone ate fish, given their proximity to the Nile. Some foods are less common today, like roasted hedgehog. They wrapped the whole hedgehog in clay and baked it. When they broke off the clay, it pulled off all the spines, and dinner was ready.

How do we know what they ate? The ancient Egyptians did not write down their recipes in hieroglyphs. They did have pictures of food and left food in tombs. Some of the oldest honey in the world was found in Tutankhamun's tomb. It was still edible! Scientists have studied mummies. They can tell that most Egyptians had a nutritious diet. They can also tell some wealthy Egyptians had cavities from eating too much bread! Parasites in the mummies show trichinosis. That's how we know Egyptians ate pork. The Greeks and Romans also wrote about the Egyptians. And of course, we have Egyptian people today! Southern Egyptians still use many of their ancient methods and ingredients. date from around 1600 BC/BCE.

Egyptian Menu:

Breakfast:
Barley Meal Porridge: *p.16*
Cottage Cheese

Snacks:
Raisins: *p.41*
Dried Apples: *p.42*
Phoenician Flatbread: *p.65*
Hummus: *p.218*
Dried Spiced Beef: *p.71*

Dinner:
Cucumber Salad: *p.73*
Lentil Salad: *p.90*
Falafel: *p.86*

Dessert:
Tiger Nut Cookies: *p.169*

Drink:
Grape Juice: *p.196*

Fruits and Nuts:
Almonds
Apples
Apricots
Canteloupe
Dates
Figs
Grapes
Honeydew
Plums
Pomegranates
Watermelon

EGYPT

Tigernut Cookies

Tigernuts have been found in an Ancient Egyptian tomb dating back to 5000 BC/BCE. The tomb of Vizier Rekhmire, from c. 1400 BC/BCE depicts the making of triangular tiger nut sweets. They are sweetened with honey, which was believed to come from the tears of the sun god Re. As tigernuts and tigernut flour are expensive, you can substitute almond flour. Allergen note: tiger nuts are actually a tuber, not a true nut, and are safe for those with nut allergies.

GF; DF; V

12 Cookies

Level of
Difficulty: 2

30 minutes

Ingredients:

1 ¼ cup tiger nut flour (150g) or almond flour (125g)

1 teaspoon cinnamon

¼ cup honey + 1 tablespoon

3 tablespoons olive oil

1 egg

Ingredients Tip:
Tigernut flour is available on Amazon.

Directions:

1. Preheat oven to 325 degrees and grease a baking sheet.

2. Stir together the flour and cinnamon until combined.

3. Add 1/4 cup honey and olive oil and stir thoroughly.

4. Fold in the egg until it is fully incorporated and the mixture holds together.

5. Scoop about two tablespoons of dough onto the baking sheet and press into a ½ inch thick triangle with wet hands.

6. Repeat with the remaining amount of dough, leaving about an inch of space between each cookie.

7. Bake for 20 minutes, until golden around the edges. Those baked with almond flour will be completely golden and just brown around the bottom edge.

8. Let cool for five minutes then remove to a wire cooling rack.

9. Brush with remaining honey while still warm.

JAPAN

Jomon Chestnut Cookies

At the Ondashi Jomon site in Japan, archaeologists found preserved ancient cookies. They were able to determine that the cookies were made of chestnut flour, walnut flour, wild bird eggs, and wild boar meat and blood. They were decorated with beautiful patterns. This version has more modern ingredients and is sweet instead of savory.

GF variation, V

16 cookies

Level of
Difficulty: 2

20 minutes

Ingredients:

5 ounces shelled roasted chestnuts *(about 1 pound in the shell)*

½ cup butter, melted and cooled slightly

½ cup sugar

2 eggs

1 teaspoon vanilla

1 ½ cup flour

Ingredients Tip:
Feel free to use prepackaged peeled chestnuts or roast your own. See pg.47 for roasted chestnuts recipe.

Equipment Note
If you do not have a food processor, you can combine the melted butter, chestnuts, eggs, and vanilla in a blender. Whisk together the flour and sugar, then stir in the wet ingredients.

Directions:

1. Preheat oven to 350 degrees and grease a baking sheet.

2. In a food processor, grind the nuts into crumbs.

3. Add the melted butter and pulse to combine.

4. Add the sugar, egg, and vanilla and run for about a minute until the mixture is smooth.

5. Add the flour and run for about one more minute. The mixture should start to form into a ball.

6. Use a tablespoon to scoop balls of dough onto the cookie sheet, about 2 inches apart.

7. Grease the bottom of a drinking glass or measuring cup and use it to press the cookies into discs.

8. Use a toothpick to carve designs such as spirals into the cookies.

9. Bake for 12-16 minutes, until they start to turn golden brown around the edges.

Gluten Free Variation:
Substitute gluten free flour.

Greek Gastris

Gastris is the nutty ancestor of today's baklava, with alternating layers of sesame and nuts soaked in honey. The book containing the original recipe was called *The Art of Making Bread* and was written by an ancient foodie named Chrysippus of Tyana. That book is lost but quoted in the writings of another Greek named Athenaeus. We've simplified the original recipe but here it is for comparison:

"In Crete they make a kind of cheesecake which they call gastris. And it is made thus:— Take some Thasian and Pontic nuts and some almonds, and also a poppy. Roast this last with great care, and then take the seed and pound it in a clean mortar; then, adding the fruits which I have mentioned above, beat them up with boiled honey, putting in plenty of pepper, and make the whole into a soft mass, (but it will be of a black color because of the poppy;) flatten it and make it into a square shape; then, having pounded some white sesame, soften that too with boiled honey, and draw it out into two cakes, placing one beneath and the other above, so as to have the black surface in the middle, and make it into a neat shape." Athenaeus, The Deipnosophists

GF; DF; V

16 bars

Level of
Difficulty: 2

1 ½ hours
(including rest
time)

Ingredients:

8 ounces whole raw almonds (about 1 ¼ cups)

6 ounces or 1 ½ cups toasted sesame seeds

2 tablespoons poppy seeds

½ cup honey

Special Equipment:
Food processor or mortar and pestle

Directions:

1. Preheat the oven to 350 degrees. Spread the almonds on a baking sheet and roast for 5 minutes. Let cool briefly.

2. Grease an 8 x 8 baking dish.

3. In a food processor or mortar and pestle, grind the sesame seeds finely.

4. Process the almonds in a food processor until fine or chop them as finely as you can by hand.

5. Stir together the almonds and poppy seeds.

6. Microwave the honey for one minute.

7. Stir half of the honey into the sesame seeds and the other half into the almond and poppy seed mixture.

8. Divide the sesame mixture in half. Use a spatula to spread half the mixture in the bottom of the pan and press smooth.

9. Spread the almond-poppy seed mixture on top of the sesame layer and press down.

10. Spread the remaining sesame mixture on top and press smooth.

11. Let set for 1 hour and then cut immediately into sixteen pieces and serve.

Mesopotamian Mersu

No exact recipe survives for mersu, but we have an ancient receipt that gives us a clue:
"120 liters of dates and 10 liters of pistachios for making mersu." The receipt was for items delivered to the court of Mesopotamian King Zimri-Linn. Scholars still debate whether mersu was a cake or something else. This version is inspired by traditional Iraqi confections like Madgooga. Could this recipe have been passed down for thousands of years?

GF; DF; V; V+

1 dozen

Level of
Difficulty: 2

10 minutes

Ingredients:

1 cup pitted dates

1 cup shelled roasted and salted pistachios

Special Equipment:
Food processor (optional)

Directions:

1. Mince the dates with a knife and put into a medium bowl

2. Mince the pistachios as small as you can. You can also grind them in a food processor.

3. Use your hands or a food processor to combine the dates and pistachios until you can squeeze the mixture and it holds together. If it's not sticky enough, add more minced dates.

4. Breaking off a small amount of the mixture, roll it into ping-pong ball sized spheres.

Phoenician Cookies

The Phoenicians didn't leave behind any evidence about their desserts, but the Greeks have a traditional honey-soaked cookie called "Finikia" that they say came from the Phoenicians. Greeks today debate the exact nature of a Ānikia. These sticky honey cookies can be baked or deep fried, but some Greeks say that the baked version is called melomakarona. The oranges are part of the traditional Greek recipe but would have been unknown to the Phoenicians.

GF Variation; DF; V, V+

25 cookies

Level of Difficulty: 3

60 minutes

Ingredients:

For the cookies:

¾ cup olive oil

6 tablespoons orange juice

¼ cup sugar

¼ cup walnuts, crushed

2 teaspoons honey (vegan if desired)

1 teaspoon orange zest

2 cups (240g) flour

1 ¼ teaspoons baking powder ½ teaspoon baking soda

½ teaspoon salt

¼ teaspoon ground cloves

¼ teaspoon ground cinnamon

For the syrup:

The peel of one orange, cut into long strips

1 ½ cups sugar

1 ½ cups honey (vegan if desired)

1 ½ cups water

Directions:

1. Put all the syrup ingredients to a saucepan and bring to a boil on medium high heat.

2. Boil for 1 minute then remove from heat.

3. Strain the syrup into a bowl and put in the refrigerator to cool.

4. Preheat the oven to 375 degrees and line two baking sheets with parchment paper or silicone baking mats.

5. In a large bowl, whisk together the olive oil, orange juice, sugar, walnuts, honey, and orange zest.

6. In a medium bowl, whisk together the Āour, baking powder, baking soda, salt, ground cloves, and ground cinnamon.

7. Stir the dry ingredients into the wet ingredients, stirring until just combined. Do not overwork the dough.

8. Scoop out one tablespoon of dough and shape into an oval disc on the baking sheet. Repeat, keeping the cookies 2 inches apart.

9. Use the tines of a fork to impress lines into the tops of the cookies.

10. Bake for 10-15 minutes, until the cookies are golden brown.

11. While the cookies are baking, line a rimmed baking sheet with parchment paper or a silicone baking mat.

12. While the cookies are still warm, drop them one at a time into the cooled syrup for about 30 seconds. Take them out with a slotted spoon and put them on the rimmed tray. Be careful to avoid oversoaking them as they will fall apart.

Fig Cookies

The Hebrew Bible is the main source of our information about the diet of the Israelites. Many food items are listed in its pages. One biblical story describes a woman named Abigail who made fig cakes to placate an angry King David. These simple fig cookies are inspired by Abigail's fig cakes.

Ingredients:

GF; DF; V; V+

About a dozen cookies

Level of Difficulty: 2

2.5 hours

20 dried mission figs

6 ounces almonds

Special Equipment:
Food processor

Directions:

1. Soak the figs in a bowl of warm water for 2 hours.

2. Drain the figs and put in the bowl of a food processor with the almonds.

3. Process until the mixture holds together.

4. Preheat the oven to 200 degrees and lightly grease a baking sheet.

5. Scoop out a heaping tablespoon of the mixture and shape into a ball with your hands. Press flat. Leave a small space between each cookie on the baking sheet.

6. Bake for two hours and allow to cool.

Tzoalli: Amaranth Bars

Amaranth is a tiny seed with a mighty history. It grows all over the world, in many types of environments. The people of Mesoamerica began growing amaranth around 4000 BC/BCE. We don't know exactly how they prepared the tiny seeds, but Aztec traditions give us a clue. The Aztecs used amaranth and honey to sculpt images of the god Huitzlipochtli that were eaten as part of religious ceremonies. Today, Mexicans still make a similar dish called alegria or "joy."

GF; DF; Vegetarian

8 bars

Level of Difficulty: 1

10 minutes + rest time

Ingredients:

1 cup amaranth seeds

1 cup honey

1 teaspoon vanilla extract

¼ teaspoon salt

Directions:

1. Line an 8x8 baking dish with parchment or wax paper.

2. Heat a medium pot over medium high heat for several minutes. Make sure you have a lid for the pot.

3. Add a couple of seeds to the pot. If they pop like popcorn immediately, the pan is hot enough. Add a tablespoon of seeds and put the lid on. Continually shake the pot on the burner to keep the seeds moving and listen to them popping. When the sound starts to slow down, remove the lid. Most of the seeds should have popped. It takes 15-30 seconds. Be careful not to burn the seeds. Pour into a medium bowl.

4. Repeat with the remaining amaranth, adjusting the heat as necessary to keep the seeds from burning. You may need to give the pot a couple of seconds to reheat for each batch.

5. Microwave the honey for 45 seconds.

6. Stir the vanilla and a pinch of salt into the hot honey.

7. Pour the honey mixture over the popped amaranth and stir thoroughly.

8. Firmly press the mixture into the prepared pan and let it set for about 30 minutes.

9. Cut into 16 bars.

10. The bars can be stored in an airtight container for up to a week.

Cherry Ossetian Pie

GF variation, V

2 pies

Level of
Difficulty: 3

3 hours

While we don't have records of any Scythian desserts, cherry is one traditional filling for Ossetian pies. Feel free to use the Ossetian dough recipe or prepared pizza dough in this recipe. Just make sure to roll it very thin! This dough recipe makes two cherry pies.

Ingredients:

Dough:
3 cups (450g) all-purpose flour plus more for dusting
2 ¼ teaspoons instant yeast *(1 packet)*
2 teaspoons salt
2 teaspoons sugar
1 cup warm water *(about 110 degrees)*
½ cup sour cream
1 egg
2 tablespoons olive oil
4 tablespoons butter

Filling:
1 (15 ounce can) sour cherries
3 tablespoons sugar
3 tablespoons cornstarch
¼ cup cold water

Directions for filling:

1. Pour the cherries and their juice into a medium saucepan. Add the sugar and bring to a boil over medium high heat.

2. Whisk together the cold water and cornstarch.

3. Stir the cornstarch mixture into the cherries. Simmer until thickened.

Directions:

1. Mix together the flour, yeast, salt, sugar, water, sour cream, and egg. This works best with a mixer and paddle attachment, but can be done by hand. Mix together until everything is thoroughly combined and the dough is pulling away from the sides of the bowl. Then mix in the oil.

2. If the mixture is sticky, add additional flour a tablespoon at a time, mixing in between.

3. Turn the mixture out onto a floured surface. Form a ball with your hands and then fold it in half and press down. Rotate the dough halfway and repeat. Continue until the dough feels stretchy.

4. Put the dough in a greased bowl. Cover with a clean towel and let it rise in a warm place (70 degrees or warmer) for about 2 hours. It is done when it springs back after being pressed with a finger. Prepare fillings while the dough is rising.

5. Preheat oven to 450 degrees. Grease a baking sheet.

6. On a floured surface, divide the dough in half. Flatten the dough into a disc about 14" across.

7. Scoop the filling into the center of the dough.

8. Bring in one edge of the dough, folding it over the filling, and repeat, going around the edge.

9. When the filling is completely covered, carefully press down and flatten the filled dough until it is about a ½ inch thick.

10. Carefully transfer to a baking sheet.

11. Repeat for the second half of the dough.

12. Bake in the oven for 20-30 minutes, until golden brown. While the pies are baking, melt the butter.

13. Remove the pies from the oven and brush all over with melted butter. Let rest for five minutes and serve hot.

Gluten Free Variation

You can use gluten-free pizza dough and achieve a similar effect. Gluten-free flour cannot be substituted 1 to 1 in this recipe. Wholly Gluten Free Pizza Dough works very well.

Champurrado

Ancient Mesoamericans mixed chocolate with corn gruel to serve at special occasions such as weddings. This traditional Mexican atole (masa porridge) pays homage to these ancient peoples. The original would not have included milk, which wasn't available until after the Spanish introduced cattle.

GF; V

6 servings

Level of Difficulty: 3

20 minutes

Ingredients:

½ cup masa harina

4 cups water

1 cup milk

3 ½ ounces dark chocolate, broken into pieces *(100g, about 1 ½ cups dark chocolate chips)*

¼ cup agave nectar

⅛ teaspoon salt

Directions:

1. In a saucepan, whisk together the masa and water until no lumps remain.

2. Bring to a boil over medium heat, then reduce to a simmer.

3. Whisk in milk, chocolate, agave, and salt until the chocolate is melted.

4. Simmer, whisking constantly for 5 minutes.

5. Taste, adding more agave or salt if needed. Texture should be smooth.

6. Serve hot.

Roman Libum: Honey Cheesecake

This recipe was written down by Cato the Elder, great-grandfather to one of Julius Caesar's enemies (Cato the Younger). Libum was used as a household offeringtothegodsandheincludedthedirectionsinafarmingmanual.In his (translated) original words: "Bray 2 pounds of cheese thoroughly in a mortar; when it is thoroughly macerated, add 1 pound of wheat flour, or, if you wish the cake to be more dainty, ½ pound of fine flour, and mix thoroughly with the cheese. Add 1 egg, and work the whole well. Pat out a loaf, place on leaves, and bake slowly on a warm hearth under a crock." Don't worry, we have some easier to understand directions for you!

GF variation, V

1 small loaf

Level of Difficulty: 2

1 hour 15 minutes

Ingredients:

1 cup ricotta cheese

1 egg

34 cup flour *(roughly)* with more for flouring

1 bay leaf

2 tablespoons honey

Directions:

1. Preheat the oven to 425 degrees Fahrenheit and grease a cookie sheet.

2. Whisk together the ricotta and egg until smooth.

3. Add 1 tablespoon of flour at a time, stirring until the dough comes together into a loose ball that you can pick up with floured hands. Pat into a round loaf shape.

4. Place a bay leaf on the cookie sheet and lay the loaf on top.

5. Bake for approximately 25-30 minutes, until the loaf is firm to the touch and golden brown on top.

6. While the loaf is still hot, slice the top with an x and pour honey into the cuts.

Gluten Free Variation:

Substitute gluten free flour.

INDIA

Shrikhand

The people of India might have invented the art of fermented dairy products and have eaten dahi, a yogurt like product, for five thousand years or more. Dahi shows up in sacred texts like the Vedas and the Upanishads, as well as in religious rituals. When the dahi is strained and the whey poured off, the thicker product is called chakka. Starting around 400 BC/BCE, cooks started mixing chakka with powdered sugar (invented around the same time), spices, and nuts to make something called shikhrini. Today, the dish is called shrikhand and is served either as a side dish or a dessert. This recipe uses Greek yogurt instead of chakka, but you could also make your own yogurt (see p.58) and strain it until thick.

V, GF, V+, DF Variation

2 servings

Level of
Difficulty: 2

40 minutes

Ingredients:

¾ cup Greek yogurt

¼ cup powdered sugar

¼ teaspoon ground cardamom

5 cashews, finely chopped

5 almonds, finely chopped

5 pistachios, finely chopped

5-6 saffron threads infused in 1 tablespoon hot milk *(optional)*

Pomegranate seeds, cubed mango, or other fresh fruit *(optional)*

Directions:

1. In a medium sized bowl, gently stir together the yogurt and sugar until the sugar is dissolved. Do not stir too hard or the mixture will become liquidy. If using saffron infused milk, add with the sugar.

2. Stir in the cardamom and nuts.

3. Chill for at least 30 minutes or up to 2 days.

4. Garnish with fresh fruit as desired.

Dairy Free/Vegan Variation

Substitute coconut yogurt and reduce powdered sugar to 2 tablespoons. Taste before adding other ingredients and add another tablespoon of sugar if desired. Use water instead of milk to infuse saffron if desired.

Gingered Pears

In ancient China, fruit was a popular dessert. Asian pears have been grown in China for over three thousand years. Around the time that India learned to reĀne sugar cane into crystallized sugar, they had an active trade relationship with China. Likewise, ginger and apricots have been consumed in China since ancient times. Today, sweetened steamed or boiled pears are a popular Chinese home remedy for cough relief. We created this recipe in honor of thousands of years of Chinese food traditions.

GF; DF; V; V+

2 pears

Level of
Difficulty: 3

30 minutes

Ingredients:

2 pears *(Asian, Bosc, or Anjou)*

1 ½ tablespoons sugar

1 inch ginger root, peeled and sliced

6 dried apricots, diced

1 cinnamon stick

1 ½ cups water

Directions:

1. Cut each pear into quarters and carefully slice away the core. Cut each quarter in half so that you have eighths.

2. Add the pears, sugar, ginger, apricots, and water to a medium pot.

3. Bring to a boil then reduce to a simmer, uncovered, for 15-20 minutes, until the pears are tender.

4. Serve warm or cold depending on the season.

DRINKS

KUSH (ETHIOPIA) AND
ABORIGINAL AUSTRALIA

Berz:
Honey Water

Honey wine, called tej, is a popular meal accompaniment in Ethiopia today. Berz is the non-alcoholic version, made simply with honey and water. Across the ocean to the east, Aboriginal Australians also mixed honey and water for a sweet and refreshing drink.

GF, DF, V | 1 quart | Level of Difficulty: 1 | 1 hour

Ingredients:

4 cups water
4 tablespoons honey

Directions:

1. Pour the honey into a jar and cover with water.

2. Stir well, then add a lid and shake until the honey is dissolved.

3. Refrigerate for at least an hour, but overnight is better.

4. Serve cold or over ice.

Posca

Ah, posca. It's basically the original sports drink. Vinegar has electrolytes in it, perfect for Roman soldiers marching on campaign under Julius Caesar. While mentioned in several ancient sources, there is no mention of sweeteners. However, adding honey makes it much more palatable. Since the Romans loved sweet and sour flavors mixed together, I'm sure they would not object to the addition.

GF; DF; V; V+

1 serving

Level of Difficulty: 1

<5 minutes

Ingredients:

1 cup cold water

2 tablespoons red wine vinegar

1 tablespoon honey (optional)

Directions:

1. Stir together all ingredients in a glass.

2. Drink!

KUSH (ETHIOPIA)

Biyo Cambe: Mango Juice

Today, biyo cambe is a popular summer drink in Somalia. Although this drink is called mango juice, it's more like a smoothie. It's similar to the mango lassis popular in India. Mangos were grown in East Africa by 400 AD/CE, but perhaps the traders in Punt had a taste of this Indian Ocean fruit prior to that date.

  GF; V

 4 cups

 Level of Difficulty: 1

 5 minutes

Ingredients:

12 ounces frozen mango chunks

1 ¼ cup milk

1 cup plain yogurt

Honey *(optional)*

Special Equipment:
Blender

Directions:

1. Combine all ingredients in a blender and blend until smooth.

2. Taste and add honey to sweeten if desired. Blend again.

MESOPOTAMIA, MEDITERRANEAN,
CHINA, JAPAN

Homemade Grape Juice

People have been drinking grape wine since at least 6000 BC/BCE. Of course the first step in making wine out of grapes is to make grape juice. Then, the mixture is fermented. In this process, yeasts digest the sugars in the juice and turn them into alcohol. Homemade grape juice is delicious and refreshing, no fermentation required! You can drink it raw after it has been strained or cook the juice which will make it taste more like store bought juice. We preferred the flavor of the cooked juice. Which do you like better?

GF; DF; V, V+   1 ½ to 2 cups   Level of Difficulty: 1 or 3   1 to 1.5 hours

Ingredients:

1 pound red or black seedless grapes removed from stems

1 cup water

2 tablespoons sugar *(optional)*

Special Equipment:
Blender

Directions:

1. Rinse the grapes thoroughly and add to a blender.

2. Add the water and sugar if using.

3. Blend on high until only small flecks of skin remain.

4. Strain the mixture. A cheesecloth or flour sack cloth in a strainer works best.

5. If you want to drink it raw, stop here. You can also let the juice rest so that any sediment falls to the bottom.

6. To cook the juice: bring to a simmer in a small saucepan. Simmer for about ten minutes, until it has reduced by about ¼ cup.

7. Chill in the refrigerator for about an hour. Serve.

INDIA

Shikanji Nimbu Pani

Shikanji or Nimbu Pani is an ancient form of lemonade or limeade, popular to this day in India and Pakistan. The spices vary from recipe to recipe. You might be surprised to see cane sugar in this recipe. Indians domesticated sugarcane about 6000 years ago. At Ārst, they used a syrup made from the juice of the plant. They started crystallizing sugar a little over two thousand years ago.

GF, DF; V; V+

1 quart

Level of
Difficulty: 1

5 minutes

Ingredients:

1 large lime or 2 small limes

2 ½ cups cold water

2 tablespoons sugar

⅛ teaspoon salt

⅛ teaspoon ground cumin

Ice

Directions:

1. Juice the limes.

2. Mix the lime juice, water, sugar, salt, and cumin in a jar.

3. Put the lid on the jar and shake well.

4. Pour over ice to serve.

5. Refrigerate for up to 2 days.

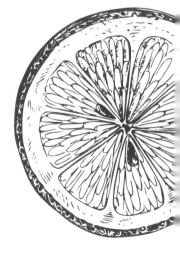

Food in Ancient West Africa

While we don't have written recipes from the Ghana Empire, we have a rich culinary tradition to draw from. West African cuisine varies from culture to culture, but has some common elements. Today, it is often spicy. During the terrible days of the Transatlantic Slave Trade, new plants arrived from the Americas. Chili peppers added spice. Peanuts replaced the indigenous groundnut. Maize (corn) is part of many more recent traditional dishes. And yet, ancient grains including millet, barley, wheat, and sorghum continue to play an important role. You might think that rice, another important grain, came from Asia. Africa actually has its own wild rice. It was domesticated in West Africa by 1000 BC/BCE.

Far from developing in isolation, the food of the Ghana Empire was the product of trade with far-off lands. The Phoenicians engaged in trans-Saharan trade for hundreds of years. They worked with nomadic Berbers as intermediaries. Sub-Saharan

Africa was part of a vast trade network. It connected southern Europe, the Middle East, and the Indian Ocean. Ingredients like chickpeas traveled across the desert. West Africa had its own native ingredients. Farmers grew cowpeas, which are like black-eyed peas, and sesame. Yams are another indigenous vegetable. They remain important in African cooking to this day.

Along with vegetables, animals traveled across the desert. The only domesticated animal native to Africa is the guinea fowl. Hunting made up an important part of the diet across the continent. Gradually, many cultures took up cattle herding. People in many West African cultures also ate sheep and goats. Chickens, which came from Asia, didn't arrive in the area until late in ancient times.

Historic Note: Archaeologists have only recently begun to study the history of agriculture in West Africa. It is also harder to find intact artifacts because of the hot and humid climate. Hopefully, this list of fruits and nuts will grow longer as archaeologists make more discoveries.

How do we know
what they ate?
Through trade, Ghana
had contact with the
Mediterranean and the
Middle East. Foreign
visitors wrote about
their trips to the Ghana
Empire.

West Africa Menu:

Breakfast:
Hausa Koko (Millet Porridge): *p.21*
Akara: *p.37*

Snacks:
Millet Flatbread: *p.61*

Dinner:
Cowpeas and Plantains: *p.81*
Chicken Yassa: *p.139*

Dessert:
Fried Plantains: *p.45*

Drink:
Ginger Juice: *p.200*

Fruits and Nuts:
Lemons
Plantains
Watermelon

Gnamakoudji: Ginger Juice

My neighbor from Sierra Leone introduced me to this spicy and delicious refreshment. She lets her ginger infuse overnight. According to my neighbor, you can use either lemon juice or lime juice. This is a traditional drink in many West African countries, and might have been around in the late days of the Ghana Empire.

GF; DF; V, V+   1 ½ to 2 cups   Level of Difficulty: 1 or 3   1 to 1.5 hours

Ingredients:

4 ½ cups water, divided

4 ounces ginger, peeled and sliced into ½ inch pieces

1 lemon, sliced thinly

2 tablespoons lemon juice

⅔ cup sugar

Special Equipment:
Blender

Ingredients Tip:
Do not substitute ground ginger for fresh ginger in this recipe.

Directions:

1. Add the ginger and ½ cup of water to a blender. Blend until smooth.

2. Boil 4 cups of water on the stove or in the microwave.

3. Carefully pour over the ginger mixture.

4. Add the lemon slices and lemon juice. Infuse for one hour.

5. Strain the mixture through a cheesecloth. Do NOT squeeze.

6. Stir in the sugar.

7. Serve chilled or over ice. Shake if the mixture settles.

PERU

Chicha Morada: Two Ways

Chicha Morada is a traditional Peruvian drink dating back to the pre-Columbian era. We don't know its exact origins or ingredients, but today's version is based on a 17th century Spanish recipe. By then, other ingredients from the Caribbean and Europe had made their way into this traditional corn drink. We have included the traditional Peruvian version and a historically-possible version. Be aware: this juice stains!

GF; DF; V; V+

½ Gallon

Level of Difficulty: 3

1 hour

Ingredients:

1 pound purple corn

1 gallon water

3 cinnamon sticks

5 whole cloves

1 pineapple, peeled, cored, and diced. Reserve peels and core.

1 ½ cups sugar

½ cup lime juice

Ingredients Tip:
The purple corn is available at international markets that stock Latin American groceries. The dried corn is sold either on the cob or loose.

Directions:

1. In a large pot, combine the corn (including cobs), water, spices, and pineapple peels and core.

2. Bring to a boil then reduce to a simmer for 45 minutes.

3. Carefully taste and add sugar. Bring back to a boil until the sugar is dissolved.

4. Allow to cool to room temperature.

5. Strain the mixture into a pitcher and stir in the lime juice.

6. Serve in a glass with ice and the diced pineapple.

Historically Possible Chicha Morada

Ingredients:

1 pound purple corn

10 cups cold water

2 passion fruits

1 cup sugar (optional and not historically accurate)

Directions:

1. Add the corn kernels (and cobs if using) and water to a large pot.

2. Slice the passion fruits in half and scoop out the pulp and seeds.

3. Add the pulp and seeds to the pot with the corn and water.

4. Bring to a boil and then reduce to a simmer for 45 minutes

5. Taste carefully and add sugar if desired.

6. Bring back to a boil until the sugar is dissolved.

7. Allow to cool to room temperature.

8. Strain and serve in a glass over ice.

Koumiss: A Modern Take

V, GF, V+, DF variation

Described by Marco Polo as a "pleasant milk drink," the original koumiss (kumiss) was made of fermented mare's milk. Carbon dioxide from the fermentation process turned the milk into a sparkling alcoholic beverage. Don't worry, this modern version is non-alcoholic and uses regular cow's milk yogurt. No mares necessary.

2-3 servings

Level of
Difficulty: 1

5 minutes

Ingredients:

½ cup Greek yogurt

3 tablespoons lemon juice

⅓ cup sugar

2 cans seltzer water, chilled

Directions:

1. Whisk together the yogurt, lemon juice, and sugar.

2. Strain the yogurt mixture into a jar. It will keep for up to a week in the refrigerator.

3. To serve, mix ¼ cup of the yogurt mixture with ¾ cup seltzer water.

Vegan/Dairy Free Variation

Substitute coconut yogurt for Greek yogurt and reduce sugar to 3 tablespoons.

SCYTHIANS

Kefir

Koumiss was made of fermented mare's milk. The closest thing today is kefir. You can find a quick modern take on koumiss on p.202, but if you want to make something closer to the original, here is the recipe. Many people use kefir grains to culture their kefir. These grains have to be cared for over time.

GF; Vegetarian

1 quart

Level of
Difficulty: 1

18 hours

Ingredients:

1 packet dehydrated kefir starter
culture

4 cups milk

Ingredients Tip:

For those new to fermentation, we recommend using dehydrated kefir starter culture which is easier to handle. These cultures can be ordered online. Generally, the culture can be reused several times according to packet directions.

Directions:

1. Pour 4 cups of milk into a glass jar.

2. Add the packet of kefir starter and stir gently.

3. Cover with a coffee filter or cloth. Do NOT put a lid on the jar.

4. Let sit for 12-18 hours in a warm place (72-74 degrees)

5. It will be as thick or thicker than heavy cream when finished and taste like yogurt.

Note: Some people make kefir with coconut milk, coconut water, or juice. See your starter packet for directions.

Minthe and Persephone

Long ago, there lived a nymph named Minthe. She lived in the river Kokytos, the River of Wailing. Her river flowed into the river Acheron and that river divided the world of life from the Underworld. Hades was the god of the Underworld and knew every bit of earth beneath the ground. He fell in love with the nymph of the dark and raging river.

For a time, Minthe dwelled in the palace of the God of the Underworld and was happy. When he was oĀ doing his godly work, she wandered the gardens. But, like his brother Zeus, Hades was not a faithful man.

He spied the goddess Persephone alone in a field, and fell in love with her. Seizing her, he carried her off to his underground palac . Minthe was but a nymph and Persephone a goddess. And so, Persephone became the Queen of the Underworld. Yet, Minthe did not give up on her love so easily.

Persephone's mother, Demeter, demanded the return of her daughter. Because Persephone had eaten six pomegranate seeds, Hades argued that she must stay in the Underworld. Zeus ruled that Persephone must spend six months each year with Hades, one for each seed. The other six months, she could return to the world above and live with her mother.

Surely, with six months of the year, Minthe could convince Hades to love her once again. After all, Minthe said, "I am nobler of form and more excellent than beauty. He must banish Persephone and return to me."

But Persephone, for all she had not chosen to marry Hades, was a jealous goddess. She screamed and raged against his unfaithfulness. In her fury, she trampled the nymph into dust.

Hades mourned the loss of the nymph he had loved. He transformed her into a sweet-smelling plant that would release its perfume whenever its leaves were crushed. And so, he gave us the plant we call mint.

Because of its sweet smell, the ancient Greeks used mint in their funeral rituals to cover the smells of death.

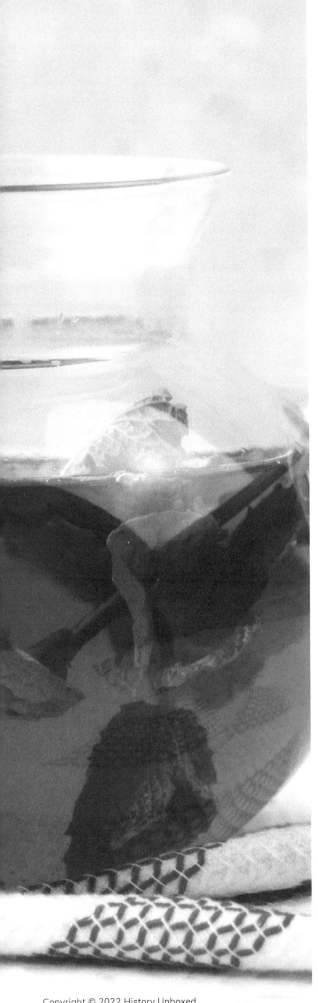

EGYPT, GREECE, ROME, NORTH AMERICA, CHINA, JAPAN, AUSTRALIA

Mint Tea

Mint is the common name for many members of the mentha genus. It grows all over the world, with species on almost every continent. Mint tea has been used as both flavoring and medicine just about everywhere it grows.

GF; DF; V, V+   1 quart   Level of Difficulty: 2   30 minutes

Ingredients:

1 ounce fresh mint leaves, washed

4 cups water

Directions:

1. Bring the water to a boil.

2. Carefully pour the boiling water over the leaves and steep for 20 minutes.

3. Strain the leaves. Drink hot or pour over ice!

Food in Ancient China

Gingered Pears

Rou Jia Mo

Cowpeas and Plantains

Shennong's Green Tea

You might think you know Chinese food. After all, almost any town of an adequate size has a Chinese take-out place. But the Chinese food at most take-out places caters to American tastes. China is an enormous country with many cultural groups, food traditions, and climates. Chinese culture stretches back thousands of years. So where did it all start?

In the north, it started with millet. In the south, it started with rice. Early people ate pork and wild game. By 2700 BC/BCE, they raised grains called the "five sacred grains." These were: barley, soy, rice, wheat, and millet. They used these grains in porridge, bread, and even noodles. The first millet noodles date back to about 2000 BC/BCE!

By the time of the Qin Dynasty, Chinese foodies had many options. Seaweed. Nectarines. Plums. Oranges and pomelos. Rice vinegar and sugar. Wine made from rice, grapes, and millet. The first cookbooks appeared during the Han Dynasty

(206 BC/BCE-220 AD/CE). They had recipes for honeyed plums, pickled vegetables, and millet mush. One grave had recipes written on 300 strips of bamboo!

During the Han Dynasty, cooks had soy sauce to flavor their chicken and duck. They ate chestnuts, cabbage, and bamboo shoots. They dried meat, steamed rice, and stir-fried vegetables in woks. They deep-fried, braised, and boiled their food. In short, you can glimpse the origins of what we think of as Chinese food. They also ate less common meats, like the elephant trunk (supposedly it tastes like pork).

How did they eat their food? Well, the oldest chopsticks date back to about 1750 BC/BCE, but most people likely ate with their hands. Chopsticks were universal by the time of the Han Dynasty.

Modern Chinese food relies on ingredients not available to ancient cooks. China is the second largest producer of corn on the planet, but that's an import from the Americas. Chinese cooks today also often use peanuts, a South American crop. Authentic Chinese food still has regional differences. Pork is still the most popular meat, except in areas with high Muslim populations. China has mountains, deserts, rivers, and forests. Each region has different local ingredients and specialties. Today, Chinese cuisine has the "Eight Cuisines." These are Anhui, Guangdong, Fujian, Hunan, Jiangsu, Shandong, Sichuan, and Zhejiang. Anhui is a simple cuisine that uses wild herbs. Guangdong, or Cantonese, style Chinese food is the most common in the United States. Fujian dishes are light and often contain seafood. Shangdong is rich and broth-based. Jiangsu food is soft-textured and seasonal. Sichuan is bold and spicy. Zheijang is fresh and mellow. All these styles are based on the traditional dishes of their provinces. Their roots stretch deep into the past.

How do we know what they ate? Written Chinese dates back over 3000 years. Although the oldest known cookbook was written around 1300 AD/CE, earlier writings give an idea of the food culture of China. The government kept records. People wrote about daily life and gave advice.

Chinese Menu:

Breakfast:
Millet Porridge: *p.21*

Snacks:
Grapes
Oranges
Pears
Peaches

Dinner:
Thunder Tea Rice: *p.91*
Rou Jia Mo: *p.157*

Dessert:
Gingered Pears: *p.191*

Drinks:
Shennong's Green Tea: *p.211*

Fruits and Nuts:
Grapes
Nectarines
Oranges
Peaches
Pears
Plums

Chinese Kitchen God

In China, thousands of years ago, there lived a man named Zhang Dan. He and his wife had been happily married for many years. But one day, his eyes fell upon a beautiful young woman in his village. He fell in love with her and begged her to run away with him.

And so Zhang Dan abandoned his faithful and loving wife for another woman. Heaven struck him blind as punishment for his sin. The beautiful young woman did not want to be married to a blind man. She abandoned him. Blind and alone, Zhang Dan had to beg for food and money just to survive.

As he begged, he came to the house where his first wife lived. In his blindness, he did not recognize her when she answered the door. She recognized him, however. When she saw her husband's face and ragged clothes, she pitied him. She invited him in and prepared him a warm bath. As he gratefully soaked in the hot water, he told her his story.

"Oh, lady. I had such a wife. I loved her but fell victim to my own passions. If I could only find her again, I would tell her how sorry I was and beg for her forgiveness." His wife immediately forgave him.

"Oh, dear husband, open your eyes! You have found her!" He opened his eyes as she bid, and found to his amazement that he could see her. When he saw her face, he was filled with a consuming guilt. He threw himself into the fireplace to punish himself. Before she could save him, the flames had claimed him. In her grief, she made a shrine to her husband over the fireplace.

Meanwhile, Zhang Dan was surprised to find that he was neither a ghost nor in Hell. He found himself in the court of Yu Huang Da Di, Jade Emperor and Emperor of the Heavens.

"You are forgiven for your past," the Jade Emperor said. "You are now Zao Jun, the Stove God." Zao Jun bowed to the floor in front of the Emperor. "You will watch over each family from their hearth. Then you will come back to me once each year and tell me all that has passed."

In reward for her faithfulness and love, Zao Jun's wife was allowed to remain with him forever. She became his scribe and wrote down all that he saw. Every year, just before the Lunar New Year, Zao Jun makes his report to the Jade Emperor.

To make sure that he makes a good report, each family cares for a statue of Zao Jun throughout the year. They make him offerings on his birthday. And just to make sure he can't say anything bad, they stuff his mouth with sweets right before he heads off to visit the Jade Emperor.

CHINA

Shennong's Green Tea

The first written records of tea drinking come from the 3rd century AD/CE, but people have been drinking tea for even longer. According to Chinese legend, Emperor Shennong discovered tea when its leaves blew into a cup of hot water he was preparing to drink. He found that he liked the taste of the leaves in his tea. Shennong is more of a man of legend than of history, but historians recently discovered tea in an emperor's tomb from 2100 BC/BCE. In tea's early history, it was likely more of a medicinal or food ingredient. But we honor the story of Shennong with a perfectly brewed cup of green tea.

GF; DF; V, V+

1 serving

Level of Difficulty: 2

15 minutes

Ingredients:

¾ cup water
1 teaspoon (2 grams) loose-leaf green tea

Directions:

1. Measure the leaves into an infuser or directly into the cup.

2. Heat the water on high just until small bubbles start to form.

3. Pour the water over the tea leaves.

4. Steep for two minutes.

5. Strain out the leaves and drink carefully.

Quetzalcoatl's Gift:
An Aztec Legend

The god Quetzalcoatl (ketz-el-ka-tel) looked down at the humans on earth who struggled to find enough food. When he saw their thin bodies and hungry faces, he pitied them and decided to help. "I shall bring them a gift," he thought to himself. When the people looked up into the sky that morning, they saw a star growing bright and brighter. With a flash, a man stood before them. They knew right away that this was no ordinary man. They built him a grand temple, five stories tall, right in the center of town, and began to worship him instead of their older idols. Quetzalcoatl taught them how to grow maize, yucca, and beans, and the people thrived. He asked Tlaloc, the rain god, and Xochiquetzal, the goddess of fertility and vegetation, to bless the people.

When the people mastered the skill of farming, Quetzalcoatl wanted to reward them with a special gift. His rival, Tezcatlipoca (tes-kaht-li-poh-kah), had a bush with delicious fruit reserved only for the gods. The bush was called xocatl. Quetzalcoatl stole the bush and gave it to the people. Tlaloc watered the bush and Xochiquetzal decorated the xocolatl bush with beautiful red flowers. When the fruit ripened, Quetzalcoatl showed the people how to remove the seeds, roast them, and crush them to make a delicious drink called xocolatl (sho-KWA-til). The people grew strong, wise, and powerful with the help of Quetzalcoatl. The other gods became jealous and asked Tezcatlipoca to punish Quetzalcoatl.

Furious at the theft of his bush, Tezcatlipoca was happy to oblige. He disguised himself as a pulque vendor, selling an alcoholic drink made from agave nectar. Tezcatlipoca found a saddened Quetzalcoatl in the marketplace.

Quetzalcoatl had learned that he was to be punished. Pretending to comfort the other god, Tezcatlipoca offered Quetzalcoatl a cup of pulque. Or perhaps two.

Quetzalcoatl's sadness disappeared, but the drink made him dance around and embarrass himself in front of the people who had worshiped him. When he awoke the next morning, he realized that they had lost respect for him and that it was time for him to leave. The gods punished him further by turning all of his beautiful xocolatl bushes into spiky cacti: the very agave plants whose fermented nectar had led to his downfall. But Quetzalcoatl had one more gift: he had one remaining xocolatl seed which he planted as he returned to the heavens to take his place as the morning and evening star. All of the xocolatl today is descended from that one special seed.

Historic Notes:

Quetzalcoatl was represented as a feathered serpent and was the god of health, love, agriculture, and food. Images of Quetzalcoatl date back to Olmec times and he was a god in many Mesoamerican cultures. This legend comes from the Aztecs. Aztec culture thrived in Mesoamerica from the early 14th century until Spanish arrival in 1521. The Aztecs were not the first Mesoamerican people to cultivate cacao, but their language, Nahuatl, gives us the word chocolate from "xocolatl." The Mayans called the bush "ka'kau," which is where we get our word cacao. Both cultures credited the gods for this marvelous plant, and indigenous peoples in Mesoamerica still use chocolate in their religious ceremonies.

Olmec Hot Chocolate

The Olmec people were the first to drink chocolate, a drink prepared from roasted and fermented cacao beans. The Olmecs, Mayans, and Aztecs all enjoyed drinking chocolate. It was a drink for the elites. The Spanish brought the drink back to Europe, adapting to European tastes by adding milk and sugar. It wasn't until the 19th century that chocolate became a food as well as a drink. This recipe is closer to the original drink. Have a taste and then add milk and sugar to taste if you prefer. You can use chopped baker's chocolate or chocolate chips. Cacao nibs would be the most authentic option, as well as being dairy free/vegan.

GF; V; DF and V+ option   1 serving   Level of Difficulty: 3   10 minutes

Ingredients:

1 ounce unsweetened or bittersweet chocolate

1 cup water

Optional additions:
Cayenne (historically accurate)
Agave nectar (historically accurate)

Directions:

1. Bring water to a boil in a small saucepan.

2. Put the chocolate in the bottom of a mug. Add about half of the boiling water and stir with a fork to dissolve the chocolate.

3. Add the rest of the water and any remaining ingredients and stir.

4. Let cool until safe to drink.

MESOAMERICA

Mexican Atole

When the Spanish arrived in Mexico, atole was already an ancient drink. We know people have been drinking a cornmeal and water mixture for thousands of years but don't have an exact date. This version benefits from the Columbian exchange with the addition of milk, cinnamon, and vanilla. For a more historically accurate version, use just water, masa harina, and agave nectar. Atole is somewhere between a porridge and a drink.

GF, V

1 quart

Level of
Difficulty: 3

20 minutes

Ingredients:

½ cup masa harina

4 cups water

1 cup milk

3 tablespoons agave nectar

1 teaspoon cinnamon

1 teaspoon vanilla extract

Directions:

1. Combine all ingredients except for the vanilla in a medium saucepan and whisk thoroughly.

2. Bring the mixture to a simmer over medium heat, stirring frequently.

3. Cook for about 10 minutes, until the mixture is smooth.

4. Remove from heat and whisk in the vanilla.

5. Serve hot.

Food Preservation

The first refrigerator for home use was invented in 1913, so how did people keep their food fresh until then?

The simplest method was still about keeping food cold. Even in prehistoric times, ancient hunter-gatherers took advantage of snow, ice, and dark, cool caves. They stored food in cold places to keep their food fresher longer. Later, people built ice houses. These partially buried structures were places where snow and ice were packed during the winter. The cool ground kept the ice from melting into the warmer months. These cool places were excellent for food storage. They also allowed fancier people to drink cool drinks in the middle of summer.

People in hot and dry climates learned they could use the heat of the sun to dry their food. Drying kept it from spoiling indefinitely. Bacteria need moisture to survive, and dehydration kills them. This practice developed independently around the world thousands of years ago. Smoking food over a fire achieved a similar outcome. Cooking also helps food keep longer, because it kills germs present in the food.

Salt, oil, vinegar, and honey were all used as preservatives. Foodstuffs packed into these materials kept much longer. Why? Keeping food away from air, light, and moisture keeps bacteria from growing. People used to say that cooks used spices to disguise the taste of rotten food. That's not true. Spices were too expensive, and people knew that rotten food made people sick, even if they didn't know about germs. Instead, spices helped balance out the salty taste of salt-preserved foods.

Fermentation is another ancient food preservation technique. It destroys microbes. In fermentation, micro-organisms like yeasts break down sugars. Then they convert them to acids or alcohols. Fermentation gives us wine and beer, but also yogurt, yeasted breads, and sauerkraut.

All these food techniques are still used around the world, and give us some truly tasty dishes!

Condiments

INDIA
Ghee

Ghee is a type of clarified butter. It was invented in India thousands of years ago. The heat in India makes regular butter turn rancid quickly, but ghee lasts for much longer. It's also great for frying. Ghee is also a part of the Hindu religious tradition. Use wherever you would use butter or cooking fats.

GF, V

2 cups

Level of
Difficulty: 3

30 minutes

Ingredients:

1 pound unsalted butter

Directions:

1. Cut the butter into cubes and place in a small saucepan on low heat.

2. When the butter is fully melted, bring the heat up slightly until the butter begins to simmer.

3. Reduce the heat if it starts to sputter, but keep simmering for about 30 minutes. The ghee is finished when the butter turns completely clear and you can see the milk solids on the bottom of the pan. They should be just starting to turn brown.

4. Let cool for five minutes then pour through a cheesecloth or coffee filter to strain out the solids.

5. Ghee keeps at room temperature for three months or in the refrigerator for a year.

EGYPT

Hummus

Chickpeas were a staple item in the ancient Egyptian diet. Today, hummus is a popular dish in Egypt, the rest of the Mediterranean, and the Middle East. The oldest known recipes for hummus date back to the 13th century, but all of its ingredients had been part of the Egyptian diet for several thousand years.

GF; DF; V; V+

2 cups

Level of
Difficulty: 2

50 minutes

Ingredients:

1 15 ounce can chickpeas, rinsed and drained

¼ cup tahini

¼ cup olive oil

¼ cup water

1 clove garlic, peeled (about 1 teaspoon minced)

¾ teaspoon salt

3 tablespoons lemon juice

Special Equipment
Food Processor

Directions:

1. Add all ingredients to the bowl of a food processor.

2. Process until smooth.

3. Chill for 30 minutes before serving.

Salt Preserved Lemons

Salt was a big deal in the ancient world: a really big deal! The salt trade in ancient Ghana is one of the things that made it so incredibly rich. In a time before refrigeration, salt was a vitally important ingredient in preserving foods like fruit, vegetables, and meats. The oldest recipe for salt preserved lemons dates back to 12th century Egypt, but references to them go back even further.

GF; DF; V; V+   4 lemons   Level of Difficulty: 2   15 minutes + 1 month curing time

Ingredients:

5 fresh lemons, washed and dried

¼ cup salt

Ingredients Tip:

1 sterilized wide mouth quart jar

Directions:

1. Slice the nubs oĀ of both ends of the lemons

2. Standing the lemon on one end, carefully slice down in quarters, leaving the quarters attached at one end.

3. Sprinkle one tablespoon of salt at the bottom of the jar and another tablespoon inside the Ārst lemon.

4. Press the lemon sliced side down into the mason jar and press down to release some juice. Repeat slicing and salting with three more lemons.

5. If you do not have enough lemon juice and salt to cover all four lemons, juice the Ānal lemon and add the juice to the jar to cover.

6. Screw the lid on tightly and store at room temperature for 30 days, shaking daily.

7. At the end of the 30 days, the lemon peels should be soft and the pulp almost dissolved. They are ready to be used in recipes!

MEDITERRANEAN

Date Syrup and Date Paste

Date syrup was used as a sweetener in the ancient Mediterranean world. Use it anywhere you would use a sweet syrup today. The leftover date paste is still delicious and can be spread on bread or stirred into porridge.

GF; DF; V; V+

1 ½-2 cups

Level of
Difficulty: 3

2 hours

Ingredients:

4 cups water

1 pound pitted dates

Special Equipment
Cheesecloth

Directions:

1. Bring the water and dates to a boil on high heat.

2. Reduce the heat and simmer for 30 minutes.

3. Strain the mixture through a cheesecloth. When it is cool enough to handle safely, squeeze the cheesecloth tightly to get out as much liquid as possible. Reserve the mashed dates.

4. *Optional: Return the syrup to the stove and boil to reduce and thicken the syrup. It will get thicker after refrigeration. You can also blend the leftover dates in a blender or food processor to make a smoother spread.*

Ahuaca-Mulli-Guacamole

The Spanish first tasted ahuaca-mulli upon meeting the Aztecs. In Nahuatl, the Aztec language, ahuacatl is the word for avocado and mulli is the word for sauce. But the Aztecs weren't the first humans to eat avocados. The people of Mesoamerica have been eating avocados for about 10,000 years. This recipe is based on that first tasted by the Spanish, but with the addition of a small amount of lime juice to keep the guacamole from oxidizing and turning brown.

GF; DF; V; V+   2 cups   Level of Difficulty: 2   5 minutes

Ingredients:

3 large or 4 small avocados

1 tablespoon lime juice

1 teaspoon salt

1 teaspoon onion powder

12 cherry tomatoes, cut into quarters

Special Equipment:

Potato masher

Directions:

1. Carefully cut the avocados in half and remove the pit. To remove the pit, dig the edge of the blade of the knife into the pit and twist until it comes free. You can also push the pit from the outside with your thumbs.

2. Use a spoon to scoop the avocado out of the peel and into a bowl.

3. Mash the avocados with a potato masher or large spoon.

4. Stir in the salt, lime juice, and onion powder. Taste and adjust seasonings if desired.

5. Stir in the cherry tomatoes.

PERU

Chavin Peanut Butter

GF; DF; V; V+

Many children enjoy peanut butter and jelly sandwiches. Peanuts are a great food because they are high in protein, easily portable, and store well. Today, people all over the world enjoy eating them. The people of Peru began to cultivate peanuts 7000 years ago (5600 BC/BCE). Just like today, they ate them roasted or as peanut butter. People made peanut-shaped pottery over three thousand years ago. Later the Incas combined peanuts and honey to make cakes. They oﬀered peanuts to their gods and buried peanuts with their mummies. Brazilian people ground peanuts and maize together to make a drink as early as 1,500 years ago. Others ground peanuts and cacao (chocolate) together.

1 ½ cups

Level of Difficulty: 1

5 minutes

Ingredients:

2 cups dry roasted peanuts

Special Equipment:
Food processor or mortar and pestle

Directions:

1. Put your peanuts in a food processor OR mortar and pestle. If using a mortar and pestle, work with ¼ cup of peanuts at a time.

2. Process or grind the peanuts until they reach the desired smoothness. It takes about 5 minutes in a food processor, but will take quite some time with a mortar and pestle.

3. Refrigerate for up to two weeks.

When Spanish conquerors arrived in Mexico, they tasted peanuts for the ﬁrst time. They thought that peanuts were delicious. Spanish and Portuguese explorers took the peanut with them back to Europe and to the other continents they visited: Asia and Africa. In Africa, the peanut had a cousin called the Bambara groundnut, but it wasn't as tasty and didn't produce as many nuts. The peanut quickly became a popular replacement. The slave ships also carried peanuts to feed the slaves onboard because they were cheap and kept well. Most historians believe that the peanut arrived in the North American British colonies by slave ship, instead of coming up through Mexico.

Today, China leads the world in peanut production. Most places use peanuts in cooking and peanut butter isn't as popular in the rest of the world as it is in the United States. However, peanut butter is popular in Canada and the Netherlands. The Netherlands imports almost half of all the peanuts in Europe! Did you know that peanuts aren't just for eating? In the 20th century, an African American scientist named George Washington Carver wrote about 300 diﬀerent uses for the peanut plant. Today, they can be found in some kinds of bleach, cosmetics, medicine, and even explosives!

Peanuts are actually not nuts at all! They are a legume, more like a pea or a bean. Unlike other legumes, which produce a bean on the end of the ﬂower, the peanut sends a stalk, called a peg, from the ﬂower down into the soil. The fruit develops underground.

PERU

Chili Pastes

These chili pastes are a traditional condiment from Peru. The panca chili paste uses ingredients available to the Chavin culture, while the Amarillo paste includes onions which were not available until they arrived with European colonizers.

GF; DF; V; V+

4 ounces of each paste

Level of Difficulty: 2-3

2 hours

For Panca Chili Paste
Ingredients:

2 dried ancho or panca chilies

½ teaspoon salt

Directions:

1. Cover the ancho chilies with water and soak for 2 hours.

2. Drain ancho chilies and puree with salt in a food processor or blender.

Tip: You can wear gloves to keep the oils from getting on your hands. If not, wash your hands very thoroughly afterwards with dish soap. Do not touch your face until you wash your hands!

For Amarillo Chili Paste:
Ingredients:

1 tablespoon olive oil

½ yellow onion, chopped

2 cloves garlic, minced

2 serrano or amarillo chilies, chopped (for less heat, remove ribs and seeds)

1 yellow bell pepper, seeds and ribs removed, chopped

Directions:

1. Heat the olive oil in a skillet until shimmering and add onions.

2. Cook onions until soft but not brown, about eight minutes. Add garlic and cook for about 30 seconds more.

3. Stir in hot and sweet peppers and cook for about 5 minutes more. Remove from heat and let cool.

4. Puree mixture in a food processor or blender.

Acknowledgements

This book would not have been possible without the help and inspiration of so many people. My dad was the first person to teach me to love cooking. He also encouraged my love of history. The Skaer family, Carr family, Schwartz family, and Takats family were fabulous recipe testers. Elizabeth Hauris, thank you for creating History Unboxed and giving me the opportunity to create this cookbook. Abigail, David, Charlotte, and Lucy, thank you for being my kitchen helpers and focus group. Abigail, your artistic direction was especially helpful. Charles, thank you for your endless support in all things, your constructive criticism, and patience with an always messy kitchen. Thank you for your creative brainstorming and the beautiful photographs that brought this food to life.

Selected Bibliography

Alcock, Joan P. *Food in the Ancient World.* Westport: Greenwood Press, 2006.

Bottéro, Jean. *The Oldest Cuisine in the World: Cooking in Mesopotamia.* Chicago: The University of Chicago Press, 2004.

Coe, Sophie D. *America's First Cuisines.* Austin: University of Texas Press, 1994.

Cox, Beverly and Martin Jacobs. *Spirit of the Harvest: North American Indian Cooking.* New York: Stewart, Tabori & Chang, 1991.

Dalby, Andrew and Sally Grainger. *The Classical Cookbook.* Los Angeles: Getty Publications, 2012.

Farnworth, Edward R. *Handbook Of Fermented Functional Foods.* London: CRC Press, 2017.

Flandrin, Jean-Louis and Massimo Montanari. *Food: A Culinary History from Antiquity to the Present.* New York: Columbia University Press, 2013.

Freedman, Paul. *Food: The History of Taste.* London: Thames & Hudson, Ltd., 2019.

Gebreyesus, Yohanis. *Ethiopia: Recipes and Traditions from the Horn of Africa.* London: Octopus Books, 2018.

Gozzini, I., Herklotz, A. and Simeti, M. *A Taste of Ancient Rome.* Chicago: University of Chicago Press, 1992.

Kaufman, Cathy. *Cooking in Ancient Civilizations.* Westport: Greenwood Press, 2006.

Höllmann, Thomas O. *The Land of the Five Flavors: A Cultural History of Chinese Cuisine.* New York: Columbia University Press, 2010.

Marks, Gil. *Olive Trees and Honey: A Treasury of Vegetarian Recipes from Jewish Communities Around the World.* Hoboken: Wiley Publishing, Inc., 2005.

Mehdawy, Magda and Amir Hussein. *The Pharaoh's Kitchen: Recipes from Ancient Egypt's Enduring Food Traditions.* Cairo: The American University in Cairo Press, 2010.

Morse, Kitty. *A Biblical Feast: Ancient Mediterranean Flavors for Today's Table.* La Caravane Publishing, 2012.

Newton, John. *Cooking With the Oldest Foods on Earth: Australian Native Foods.* Sydney: NewSouth Publishing, 2019.

Newton, John. *The Oldest Foods on Earth: A History of Australian Native Foods.* Sydney: NewSouth Publishing, 2016.

Shaw, Thurston et al. *The Archaeology of Africa: Food, metals, and towns.* London: Routledge, 1993.

Standage, Tom: *An Edible History of Humanity.* New York: Bloomsbury, 2009.

The Story of Food: An Illustrated History of Everything We Eat. New York: DK Publishing, 2018.

Swentzell, Roxanne and Patricia M. Perea. *The Pueblo Food Experience Cookbook: Whole Food of Our Ancestors.* Santa Fe: University of New Mexico Press, 2016.

Tannahill, Reay. Food In History. Paw Prints, 2008.

Toussaint-Samat, Maguelonne. *A History of Food.* Chichester: John Wiley & Sons, Ltd., 2009.

Turner-Neale, Margaret-Mary. *Bush Foods: Arrente Foods from Central Australia.* Alice Springs: IAD Press, 1994.

Wariyaa: Somali Youth in Museums. *Soo Farista: Come Sit Down. A Somali American Cookbook.* St. Paul: Minnesota Historical Society Press, 2018.

Wrangham, Richard. *Catching Fire: How Cooking Made Us Human.* New York: Basic Books, 2009.

Quotes:

"The man with whom I do not dine is a barbarian to me."

Graffiti in ompeii

"There's no arguing about taste."

Roman saying (it means that there are no absolutes about good or bad taste).

"To eat and drink without a friend is to devour like the lion and the wolf.

Epicurus, 341-270 BC, Ancient Greek philosopher

There are only three gems on earth: water, food and sweet speech. They are fools who dig out stones and call them gems.

Chanakya, 370-280, Indian teacher & philosopher

Historical Trivia for Dessert

Did you know: Ancient peoples had chewing gum? In Australia and Ancient Greece, people chewed a type of tree resin. Some Native Americans in North America chewed sugar pine and spruce sap. The Mayans chewed a type of tree gum called chicle.

Did you know? Most ancient grains were ground using stones. That meant bread contained stone dust, which wore down teeth over time!

Did you know? Egyptians grew a relative of Romaine lettuce and used it to make love potions!

Did you know? Archaeologists found watermelon seeds in Tutankhamun's tomb?

Did you know? In Ancient Egypt, only pharaohs were allowed to eat mushrooms.

One feast in Mesopotamia lasted 10 days and served 69,754 guests! They ate: 1000 oxen; 14,000 sheep; 1,000 lambs; hundreds of deer; 20,000 birds; 10,000 fish; 10,000 jerboa; 10,000 eggs; and thousands of jugs of beer and skins of wine.

Did you know? There were at least 20 different kinds of cheese in Sumeria? They flavored them with honey or mustard, and made both soft and hard cheeses;

Did you know? In Mesopotamia, there were over 300 kinds of bread?

Did you know? The Greek gods only accepted domestic animals as sacrifices!

Did you know? The ancient Greeks had a cookbook written in poetic form?

Did you know? In ancient China, raw food was considered uncivilized!

Did you know? Herodotus, a Greek writer, claimed that "kinamomon" (cinnamon sticks) were "brought to Arabia by large birds, which carry them to their nests, made of mud, on mountain recipes which no man can climb." Another Greek writer, Theophrastus, said that cinnamon grew in glades guarded by venomous serpents. Pliny the Elder, a Roman, was a bit more practical. "Those old tales were invented by the Arabs to raise the price of their goods."

Did you know? The Romans believed that the phoenix, a mythical bird, made her nest from spices.

Did you know? Pharaoh Ramses II was buried with a peppercorn in each nostril?

Did you know? The Egyptians didn't just make paper with papyrus, they ate it too!

Did you know? The color orange is named after the fruit!

Index

Locators in **'bold'** denote pictures.

E

F

N

O

P